The Post-Carbon Economy

5 Secrets for Corporate Leadership
When Carbon is Priced

Amit Chatterjee
Jay Whitehead

First Edition Published By:
SOFICO Books
West Orange, New Jersey 2009

This book is printed on 100% post-consumer recycled paper
by Forest Stewardship Council (FSC) certified printer
Thomson-Shore, a member of both the Green Press Initiative
and the Book Industry Environmental Council (BIEC).

First edition published by SOFICO Books
263 Gregory Avenue
West Orange, NJ 07052

Printed in the United States of America

Book Web site: www.PostCarbonEconomyBook.com

Library of Congress Cataloging-in-Publication Data

Whitehead, Jay
Chatterjee, Amit

The Post-Carbon Economy: The 5 Secrets of Corporate Leadership When Carbon is Priced/ Amit Chatterjee and Jay Whitehead

Includes biographical references and index.

ISBN-13: 978-0-615-29878-8 (cloth)

1. Business. 2. Competitive Advantage. 3. Carbon accounting.
4. Industrial management—Environmental aspects.

Contents

Foreword

By Ted Schlein, Managing Partner, Kleiner Perkins Caufield & Byers

Since Al Gore's Academy Award-winning documentary *An Inconvenient Truth* debuted on May 24, 2006, innovation and investment initiatives to combat climate change have intensified. Good thing, since every day we see more scientific evidence that we are rapidly nearing the point of no return on global warming and have less time to act. And while my partner John Doerr has called it the largest economic opportunity of the 21st century, the carbon trend is not most businesses' friend. In my venture capital investing role I have argued that for the U.S. government to set a price on carbon emissions is one of the most important things we can do to propel the economy, enhance our energy security goals and help make America the worldwide leader in the next global industry. I have made several investments to back up my argument. And fortunately I am not alone.

Like you and me, authors Amit Chatterjee and Jay Whitehead are simultaneously concerned citizens and forward-focused businesspeople. They just happen to know an awful lot about how much your carbon emissions are worth. The questions they ask and answer in this book are practical. They are the day-in, day-out questions you have or will ask yourself, including "How can I best compete when carbon emissions are about to cost me and my competitors real money?"

The Post-Carbon Economy does something rare. In it, co-authors Amit Chatterjee and Jay Whitehead boldly claim that to a much larger level than ever before, this century's corporate leaders will be judged, will be ranked, and will need to compete on environmental business metrics. All of a sudden, measures such as carbon efficiency matter. That is because looking forward, winning companies will be those with the greatest ability to measure, manage, and minimize their carbon emissions.

This book, perhaps for the first time, creates a model for competitive advantage in an era when carbon costs are mandated on the broadest-ever group of companies. While avoiding preference for one carbon regulatory regime over another, Chatterjee and Whitehead illustrate how government-imposed costs to cure climate change create a changed playing field for corporations large and small. They have looked around the corner. They see a new commercial reality. In *The Post-Carbon Economy*, they see that cutting carbon creates capital.

Back in 1993, Paul Hawken's pioneering book *Ecology of Commerce* created the language of what we now know as sustainability. And it provided many, including carpet square inventor Ray Anderson, a "spear in the chest" inspiration to re-invent their companies around sustainable practices. Fast-forward a decade and Al Gore's *An Inconvenient Truth* gave the world the vision to see the dangers of climate change, and start to act accordingly.

This book, *The Post-Carbon Economy*, gives you and your fellow corporate leaders a pair of carbon-colored glasses, allowing you to see how carbon costs transform your day-to-day business landscape. What you see might scare you. It might inspire you. Either way, you owe it to yourself and your business to read *The Post-Carbon Economy* and learn what it will take to compete when carbon costs money.

Menlo Park, California
August 2009

Introduction

This is the one fact you need to know. Within the next decade, $1 trillion (with a "t") in carbon emission-reduction costs will hit our economy. Your job is to figure out how to handle your share while continuing to compete in your market.

Our goal with this, the first edition of *The Post-Carbon Economy*, is to prepare you to survive and thrive when these staggering costs rain down on your organization. Is $1 trillion in added costs manageable? It is when we consider two data points. First, the all-in cost of the cure for the 2008–2009 debt crisis is over $2 trillion. And despite incurring this cost burden, the American economy is still the world's largest by far. Second, to allow global warming to continue unabated will mean environmental catastrophe, a result so devastating that not even $1 trillion will fix it.

But the expense side of *The Post-Carbon Economy* is only one side of the ledger. The other is the upside. There will be many winners in The Post-Carbon Economy: companies and individuals who make the trend their friend. Hopefully that includes you. The fact you are reading this book means you know that on one level your livelihood depends on under-standing The Post-Carbon Economy and taking advantage of it. As Rahm Emanuel, President Obama's chief of staff, is prone to saying, "A crisis is a terrible thing to waste."

Our argument in *The Post-Carbon Economy* hinges on four interrelated observations. First, when carbon emissions costs are priced by the U.S. government, putting them on par with capital and energy and labor costs, the economics of our businesses and lives are changed forever, and our economy goes post-carbon.

Second, your ability to compete in The Post-Carbon Economy will largely hinge on how carbon efficient you are, since one way or another, these new carbon emission costs will undoubt-edly enter your business as well as that of your competitors here and abroad.

Third, your best hope to find your way to carbon efficiency is to switch from a traditional allocation-based costing regime to activity-based costing with a focus on carbon—what we call Activity Based Carbon Costing, or ABCC.

And fourth, since you already manage your business by processes, the best way for you to manage to compete on carbon efficiency is by managing each of your seven major business processes most carbon efficiently.

Here is *The Post-Carbon Economy* in one sentence: Once carbon is priced, your carbon efficiency will determine your competitiveness, ABCC will be your secret weapon, and a business process orientation will keep you managing to your optimal carbon competitive advantage.

The primary assertion of *The Post-Carbon Economy* is that by putting a firm price on a ton of CO2e emissions, the economics of virtually every product and service changes. For example, our back-of-the-envelope calculation shows that at the arbitrary price of $50 per ton of CO2e, the producer cost of a bottle of $6.00 retail-priced liquid detergent jumps by about 12 cents. That may not seem like much to you. But when the producer cost for the bottle is $2.00, that's a 6 percent hike in production costs. Not trivial.

While at press time we do not know what price the U.S. government will set on a ton of carbon, we can make certain assumptions based on strong research. It is a fact that energy expenses in most manufacturing and service industries run about 2 percent of total costs. With each incremental $10 per ton of CO_2e, production costs for manufacturers rise by between 1.0 percent and 2.5 percent. In some cases, that effectively doubles the cost of the company's energy. For service businesses, the total cost increases are less, 0.5 percent to 1.0 percent. Yet there are some wild exceptions, including cement makers, who suffer a steep 13 percent increase for each $10 per ton. We do know that the U.S. government's proposed cap-and-trade programs will involve free allowances of some portion of companies' carbon caps. Resources for the Future calculations show that free allowances of about 15 percent of a firm's emissions from fossil fuel and electricity use will be sufficient to avoid adverse impacts on shareholder value.[1]

While *The Post-Carbon Economy* involves a significant layer of additional costs, the principles we outline here open the door to sustainable economic growth for your business. What is more, in *The Post-Carbon Economy*, we outline an approach that will allow American entrepreneurs to lead a renaissance in manufacturing, technology, transportation, food, and energy, building both middle-class wealth and a new generation of U.S. millionaires and billionaires. In The Post-Carbon Economy, markets are de-carbonized, de-globalized, re-localized, re-forested, un-deforested, re-regulated, and carbon is sequestered, offset, and capped-and-traded. In The Post-Carbon Economy, including carbon costs in our accounting systems and in how we use human resources and deliver employer-sponsored healthcare results in re-employment and career changes for millions. Education systems are re-invented to meet new demands. And the American consumer lifestyle leads the world in a rapid transformation from carbon-intensive, long distance transportation-dependent, disposable and high-emission to de-carbonized, re-localized, durable, re-useable, renewable, and low-emission.

Those who deny the premises of *The Post-Carbon Economy* risk a carbon-heated global climate that dooms America's companies, currency, culture, and citizens to unsustainable shortages of resources, resulting in an inability to compete with stronger post-carbon businesses in France or Brazil or Denmark or China. Free-falling stocks of food, fish, and fossil fuels result in conflict involving countless American and international casualties. And our children and grandchildren in the U.S. and around the world will face recession-filled lifetimes that are, like in the days when American slave-owners ignored the costs of that abhorrent and unsustainable practice, nasty, brutish, and short.

Despite the fact that while dealing with the debt crisis of 2008–2009, nearly every industry started unknowingly to execute post-carbon strategies, not everyone agrees with our approach. Detractors fall in two camps. The first group of our critics says our post-carbon economics-based argument is too optimistic. They say we overstate carbon costs' role in changing the economics of business. They deride our faith in U.S. government-overseen carbon trading regimes, Chinese government support for high-temperature coal plants and mandatory carbon sequestration schemes, Canadian and British Columbian carbon taxes, and the European Union's allocation-driven trading programs to provide environmental remedy without catastrophic economic fallout. And they express doubt about the power of our business process focus and activity-based carbon cost accounting scheme to deliver both a business and environmental solution.

The second type says we are not ideologically green enough and focus too much on the necessity of having a strict business case. They would have us do more finger-wagging and using of the words "should" and "must" (they're right; we have tried hard to avoid using either word in this book). They fear that we have strayed too far from the "green economy" party line as embodied in such classics as Andy Savitz's *The Triple Bottom Line*, Daniel Esty and Andrew Winston's *Green to Gold*, and Adam Werbach's *Act Now, Apologize Later* or his newest book *Strategy for Sustainability*. They say we pay way too much heed to executives' need for immediate (or at least quarter-by-quarter) gratification, and don't stress that business must take the long view.

To all skeptics, we say The Post-Carbon Economy is undeniable, a fait accompli. In the U.S., a carbon cap-and-trade regime is on its way to being a permanent fixture on the scene. Elsewhere, mandatory emission limits, sequestration, and carbon taxes are as certain. We know from experience that without seeing a competitive advantage in it, the vast majority of business people will ignore any calls to pay the environment any heed. We have discovered that activity-based carbon cost accounting, or ABCC, is the most powerful weapon yet deployed to mobilize business leaders and rank-and-file businesspeople to find profits and competitive advantage while having a real impact on GHG-based global warming. And importantly, many businesses have started down the post-carbon path, by including the impact of carbon remediation costs into their stock prices, products, services, and business processes.

It strikes us that our children will never know business life before The Post-Carbon Economy. They will consider it quaint at best and horribly naïve at worst that we and our American elders burned anything and everything to run our machines, with no costs being attributed to the carbon emissions we created. Our offspring are much more aware than we are that with only 4.6 percent of the world's population, the U.S. uses 22 percent of its energy. To our kids, we say this: We cannot undo the carbon-blindness of the past, but we are doing what we can to leave the place livable for you.

Amit and Jay both want to thank our wives and families for donating precious family time to this production. We both have the privilege of working every day with our spouses, a post-carbon practice that includes occasional car-pooling to and from work (most often in low-emission vehicles). During the book writing process, we regularly asked ourselves which ideas we should credit to our marital counterparts. Here is our answer. We both live in community-property states. In both California (where Amit lives) and New Jersey (Jay's state), 50-50 is the law of the land. So how many of this book's good ideas came from our spouses? We'd say the better half.

We also want to thank Ted Schlein for his Foreword, all our reviewers and those who gave us quotes, especially members of the CRO Association Bob Pojasek of Harvard University and Joseph Wolfsberger of Eaton.

We thank our employers for their indulgence. However, since neither of them did any writing, we want to stop short of having them think they have any commercial rights to anything in *The Post-Carbon Economy*. A good solid "thank you" should suffice.

We also tip our cap to our designer Yvette Lucker for such quality work under the duress of unreasonable deadlines.

Finally, we want to thank you for picking this book up and reading it. We wrote it for you.

This is the first edition of *The Post-Carbon Economy*. The second edition, which will soon be released by a major publishing house, includes a vast expansion of Chapter 8—Secret 5's 7 Key Business Processes that Determine Winners and Losers in *The Post-Carbon Economy*.

Because this book is merely the printed version of a much larger conversation among thousands of sustainability-concerned business and civic leaders, we invite you to go to the book's official Web site, **www.postcarboneconomybook.com**, to add your observations and experiences to the business process chapters. If we select your online contribution and you will allow us to use it with attribution, we will list you in the second edition as a contributor. This way, you earn all the benefits of major business book authorship without all the pain of writing and rewriting 35,000 words. Go now to **www.postcarboneconomybook.com** to get in on the action.

Chapter 1

What Historical Forces Created The Post-Carbon Economy?

We wrote this book because we are recession-fatigued. The generation bracketed by our birthdays (Jay Whitehead, 1959; Amit Chatterjee, 1972) has suffered through four major financial collapses—the Mideast oil crisis of 1977, 1987's Black Monday crash, the 2000 Dot Com Collapse, and the Debt Crisis of 2008–2009.

Four recessions is more than any American generation has ever weathered. These recessions weigh on us. That, plus the fact we are both fathers who possess more than our fair share of confidence in our abilities to improve the world for our kids by keeping the drumbeat of recurring recessions from crushing our American childrens' quality of life.

We believe that *The Post-Carbon Economy* holds a key to U.S. economic recession resistance. In one fell swoop, The Post-Carbon Economy remediates climate change, cuts our destabilizing dependence on oil and gas produced by America's enemies, and blazes a wide trail for endless American commercial innovation. *The Post-Carbon Economy* is the next mega-trend. It is also a cure to our recession-fatigue.

Predictably, the next mega-trend gets a lot of its power from our economy's over-reliance on the last economic mega-trend: outsourcing.

Post-Carbon Is The New Flat

In his 2005 best-seller *The World Is Flat, A Short History of the 21st Century*, the *New York Times* writer argued that the Internet "flattened" the world, allowing IT, business process, and manufacturing work to be outsourced globally to low-cost labor markets, forever changing the face of business. Low-cost labor made everything eternally cheaper and all markets more competitive. Businesses must outsource or die. Go flat or get flattened.

As it turned out, "flat" market conditions were but a moment in time. In 1999, in India's IT and engineering sectors, wages were often a mere 8 percent to 15 percent of U.S. wages. Over the next nine years, competition among employers and limited pools of talent pushed Indian IT and engineering wages up 25 percent to 75 percent per year. And by 2008, Indian wages in these professions had risen to levels that equaled 75 percent to 90 percent of U.S. wages. Even in the down economy of early 2009, a large Hay Group survey reported that Indian wages rose at a strong 7.25 percent clip.[2] With offshore wages getting alarmingly close to onshore rates for U.S., Canadian, and UK IT talent, India's labor arbitrage advantage did a disappearing act. "Flat" fell flat, fast.

In addition, focus on labor arbitrage as a globalizing "flattener" of labor markets virtually ignored the market-expanding impact of the post-1992 financial engineering revolution. Never-before-seen financial derivatives such as collateralized debt obligations (CDOs) made credit available to "sub-prime" customers, which rapidly accelerated consumer and business purchasing cycles around the world. Like a circus mirror that distorts proportions, easy credit made global labor arbitrage's impact look bigger than it really was. What's more, the sudden availability of financing and the outsized profits it generated obscured the financially engineered risks that ultimately led to the 2008–2009 debt crisis. But once the debt spigot got turned off in 2008, demand quickly dried up. The circus mirror worked in reverse, and offshore labor cost advantages looked tiny in comparison to the negative impact of the suddenly recessionary market contraction.

Meanwhile, as globalization's labor arbitrage advantage shrank, the January 7, 2009, event the *Financial Times* called "India's Enron" brought the very real yet unspoken risk costs of offshore outsourcing into sharp focus. That day, the CEO of Indian IT and Financial Services outsourcing giant Satyam admitted to falsifying the existence of $1 billion in revenues. The revelation put Satyam's many Global 500 clients in a perilous position. They came face-to-face with the fact the computers housing their most precious data were a half a world away, entrusted to an admitted fraudster. And while Satyam customers were panicked, the scandal's largest psychological impact was on customers of Indian and offshore outsourcers other than Satyam. Suddenly, leaders of hundreds of companies who had outsourced HR, finance, accounting, IT, and other data management services to heretofore highly respected offshore providers such as Infosys, Tata, Genpact, WNS, EXL Services, Wipro, ICICI, and others, were assigning a risk premium to their offshore initiatives. And often, the risk premium was as large as the labor arbitrage cost savings, wiping out offshoring's labor cost advantage.

To make the storm perfect for the flat-world paradigm, a false premise of global labor arbitrage was that it assumed that carbon emissions represented zero cost. Today, Thomas Friedman, along with nearly every other flat-world analyst, acknowledges that the sustainability of the global economy depends on halting climate change. Fact is, moving all those cheaply produced products and service people across oceans and continents involves burning a lot of carbon-rich diesel, jet fuel, and coal. By spring 2009, with the new Obama administration actively pursuing a carbon cap-and-trade program and Congress presenting laws to create the carbon cost programs, many

CEOs and boards of directors were asking one big question: Considering the now-higher wages in India, the bursting of the debt crisis bubble, the now-clear risk premium associated with offshore outsourcing, and the obviously high carbon emissions involved, would we have outsourced in the first place, and is the world really flat?

While this book will argue that the labor arbitrage advantage touted in *The World Is Flat* is much less valid, it will point out another danger of keeping a flat-world view. Continuing to see technologically enabled global labor arbitrage as a cornerstone of competitive advantage will allow you to miss one of the biggest market-shaping opportunities of our lifetimes. For all those flat and financially engineered trees, you will be unable to see the forest. You will flat-out miss The Post-Carbon Economy.

In The Post-Carbon Economy, energy-in/carbon-out is just as important as cash-in/cash-out. In The Post-Carbon Economy, competitive advantage is driven by low carbon costs, rather than the flat-world's low labor costs or financially engineered borrowing power. In The Post-Carbon Economy, the commercial virtues of globalization, quality and availability of financing become table stakes—merely the price of staying in the game. In The Post-Carbon Economy, proximity to and control of natural resources once again becomes a significant competitive advantage, increasing the importance of China, whose government has been on a decade-long mineral rights buying spree. In The Post-Carbon Economy, instead of preaching the gospel of globalization, the management consultants and MBAs in highest demand all speak the newest business language: Carbonomics. In The Post-Carbon Economy, flat fails. Carbon efficiency is king.

But we're getting ahead of ourselves. First, let's show how recent business history has shaped what's just ahead. Next we'll explain what we mean by the phrase *The Post-Carbon Economy*. And then you'll see why we say that post-carbon is the new flat.

Putting Recent Business History in Perspective

Our reading of recent economic history shows that our generation's four recessions stemmed from two great overdependence risks: overreliance on financial leverage, and our addiction to carbon-based fuels. Other than to acknowledge the impact of the debt risk, this book is not about fixing the debt crisis—hundreds of authors cover that. This book is about carbon, costs, and competition. Specifically, how in The Post-Carbon Economy, competitive advantage for companies and nations and individuals depends on how well they deliver products and services after factoring in the very real government-imposed costs associated with carbon emissions. Carbon costs count. And they are about to become a business reality, with most developed and some undeveloped countries instituting carbon cap-and-trade or tax or emissions limits or mandatory carbon sequestration solutions to stop climate change.

We believe that Americans can avoid the next recession by doing two things:

1. Better managing debt risks, and

2. Understanding that the near-future's best, brightest, and biggest companies will be built on The Post-Carbon Economy's leading competitive advantage: the carbon efficiency of their products and services.

The Once and Future "Flat"

In Thomas Friedman's 2005 best-seller *The World Is Flat, A Short History of the Twenty-First Century*, he documented a significant, if momentary business trend. He traveled the world to document how new Internet, computer, and communications technologies allowed corporations to outsource parts of themselves to gain cost and speed advantages, which enabled rapid globalization of manufacturing and services. In his travels, he saw how information technologies figuratively "flattened" obstacles such as mountain ranges, political borders, cultural differences, and time zones, flowing manufacturing and service work to where it found the lowest-cost labor. The book wrote large what *Forbes Magazine* Publisher Rich Karlgaard in 2003 had already proclaimed "the cheap decade." Karlgaard and Friedman were both telling the story of the "labor arbitrage" trend—shifting work from high-cost markets to low-cost markets—which made products and services cheaper and easier to afford. To Karlgaard's credit, he made his "cheap decade" proclamation in real time. It took Friedman another couple years to connect the dots and look beyond "cheap" to declare it "flat."

In the "flat" world view, unless companies outsourced "non-core" high labor-cost processes to low labor-cost locations, they became uncompetitive. Bottom line, in the "flat" world, winners looked for low labor costs offshore, losers stayed expensive and local.

Now fast-forward from the "flat" world to The Post-Carbon Economy. In The Post-Carbon Economy, winners sport the lowest combined net cost of labor AND carbon emissions. Fact is, starting now, governments from the U.S. to Canada to the UK to EU to China are and will be imposing costs on companies' carbon emission levels, in the form of taxes (example: the Canadian province of British Columbia) or mandatory emissions limits or carbon sequestration (example: certain regions in China) or carbon emission "cap-and-trade" regimes (examples: UK, EU, and coming soon, the U.S.). Just as lower labor costs defined winners in Friedman's "flat" world, low carbon costs define winners in The Post-Carbon Economy.

We predict that in The Post-Carbon Economy being carbon-efficient will often mean bringing work from low-cost labor markets back closer to home. Why? Because long-distance physical transportation creates a lot of expensive carbon emissions. Making things locally can save more in carbon emission-related expense than it costs in higher local wages. As a result, The Post-Carbon Economy will often mean de-globalization and re-localization of markets, especially in manufacturing. The Post-Carbon Economy will make the world a little less flat.

For those like us who grasp pictures faster than words, here are the last four paragraphs in one image:

Exhibit 1

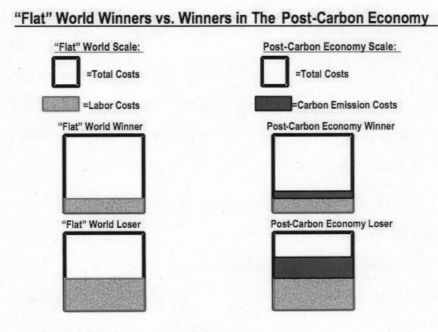

© 2009 by Jay Whitehead and Amit Chatterjee

Financial Engineering, the Debt Crisis, and Government Response

Let's get one thing straight: This book is not about the 2008–2009 debt crisis. But we cover it in summary form for one reason: The economic restructuring of 2009 enabled the emergence of The Post-Carbon Economy. The U.S. government's success in its aggressive response to the 2008–2009 debt crisis gave it license to continue being aggressive in its approach to carbon regulation. In his nearly $2 trillion in economic stimulus programs, President Obama earmarked nearly 10 percent for clean energy-related investments. In addition, the president created new taxes on offshore outsourcing, which had the effect of further un-flattening the world and spurring de-globalization and re-localization of labor markets. Flying the flag of economic recovery, the early Obama administration set the record straight that green was the new "flat."

The Internet made the lower-labor-cost "flat" world possible. But the economic boom that came before the 2008–2009 recession was not just driven by technology-enabled lower labor costs. The boom was also fueled by easy credit: financially engineered debt facilities that made it more affordable than ever to finance real estate purchases, industrial equipment, company mergers and acquisitions, and large-ticket consumer items such as autos and home improvements.

On the industrial side, GE Capital made more sales of GE airplane engines possible, and GE made more profits financing the engines than it made on the engines themselves. The same could be said for GE Capital and GE railroad engines, Ford Auto Finance and Ford cars and trucks, GMAC and GM automobiles, and Toyota Motor Credit and Toyota autos. And on the real estate and consumer credit side, new and complex financial derivatives such as Collateralized Debt Obligations, or CDOs, made home ownership possible for more people than ever before by allowing banks to "securitize" the loans and sell them to third parties, passing the loan risk to others, which simultaneously hid and multiplied the dangers of default risks by scattering them through the economy. Like low-cost labor arbitrage, which moved costs by moving work to lower-cost locations, financial engineering made products and services easier to afford. Financial engineering moved costs by pushing costs of capital out into the future and "de-risking" the debt.

On the home loan side, a larger percentage of Americans owned homes in 2006 than at any other point in America's history, largely due to relaxation of long-recognized credit qualification rules. Never since the era of credit reporting had banks offered "zero-down-payment" home loans to borrowers without requiring income verification. By late 2006, the U.S. lending industry had generated $600 billion in these "sub-prime" loans, loans extended to borrowers with less than traditional levels of qualifying income and those who had made little or no down payment.[3] The loans also often featured variable interest rates, allowed borrowers to pay interest only, and featured low "teaser" interest rates that later rose or were paid off in "balloon" payments.

So it should come as no surprise that by late 2007, a large chunk of America's "sub-prime" debt was in various stages of default. For the financial institutions who now owned "sub-prime" assets, the securities had become toxic. And while the toxicity was bad enough on its face, the negative financial impact of the "sub-prime" crisis would be magnified many times by three factors. First, new "mark-to-market" regulations required that assets such as loan securities have their market value regularly re-stated. As default rates on "sub-prime" assets climbed, the values of the toxic assets plunged, causing trading counterparties of large "sub-prime" holders such as Bear Stearns and Lehman Brothers to halt trading with them, causing a liquidity crisis on Wall Street. Second, the impact of sudden "sub-prime" asset devaluation was magnified because for the first time, loan-originating banks were able to rapidly "securitize" the loans in many forms and re-sell them to hedge funds and other financial institutions as CDOs or other securities. Often, in order to increase their potential returns, the institutions buying the troubled securitized assets had borrowed, or "leveraged up" by a ratio of 30:1, or sometimes as high as 80:1. Therefore, for every $1 in destroyed "sub-prime" asset value, buying institutions could suffer from $30 to $80 in losses. And third, as credit markets ceased up, home values started a precipitous drop. As buyers of the "securitized" loans became illiquid due to their toxic assets, banks had nowhere to sell off the loans they were originating, ran out of capital to lend, and had to stop lending. Thus, the triple-threat of toxic "sub-prime" loans, destruction of the secondary "securitization" market, and cessation of lending resulted in what we now know as the debt crisis of 2008–2009.

By mid-2008, the debt crisis had destroyed many Wall Street firms, including two icons, Bear Stearns, which was forced by the U.S. government to be acquired, and Lehman Brothers, which was pushed into bankruptcy. At the same time, the debt contagion spread to Europe, infecting the UK's largest home lender HBOS and banking leader Royal Bank of Scotland, Belgium's top lenders Fortis and Dexia, and Germany's real estate leader Hypo Real Estate, causing their governments to step in with bailouts. By late-2008, the debt crisis had also crushed the wealth of the world's stock markets, with trillions of dollars of wealth lost in mere months. By early 2009, the ceasing of the credit markets had hit U.S. employers hard, and unemployment rose precipitously, to 11.25 percent in California, America's largest state, in March 2009. The paralyzed credit markets also dragged down those industrial companies such as GE who relied so heavily on their own financing units' profits and on the units' ability to drive sales.

In 2008 and 2009, the U.S. government took unprecedented actions to remediate the debt crisis. U.S. banks were recapitalized with $700 billion in order to restimulate lending activities, which had all but halted during the worst parts of the crisis. In addition, up to another $750 billion in government guarantees were given to restimulate housing lending and home sales. U.S. government repeal of the "mark-to-market" accounting rules cut panic selling among owners of longer-term securities. While economists disagree on the wisdom of the government stimulus, they generally agree that the pre-emptive actions of both the U.S. and international governments to remedy financial market collapse stopped the recession from becoming a full-blown depression.

Growing Pains: The U.S. Service Economy, Populations, and Climate Change

An essential part of 20th century U.S. economic growth was the rapid expansion of the so-called service economy, which overtook manufacturing as America's dominant employer starting in 1900 and overtook agriculture in 1920. From 1970 to now, the United States had sent much of its manufacturing work abroad and simultaneously outsourced service support work to lower-cost developing labor markets from Mexico to China to India. This rising globalization tide floated all boats, resulting in wealth creation in the U.S., Canada, Europe, and in the developing world. With wealth creation came significant global population expansion. And with rapidly rising population came rapid increases in carbon emissions and climate change from the greenhouse effect.

Exhibit 2

35-Year Growth Curves: Service Economy, Population, Carbon Emissions

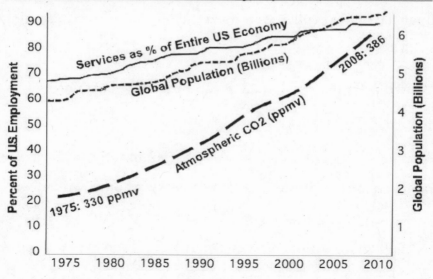

Source: Keeling Curve Data Measuring CO2 at Mauna Loa, Hawaii, JapanFocus.org/UNEP, U.S. Dept. of Commerce, Bureau of the Census

While economies boomed and countries grew, so did the scientific understanding of climate change's impacts. The main driver behind public understanding of the economic risks of human population-caused climate change was Vice President Al Gore's 2007 Academy Award-winning documentary film *An Inconvenient Truth*. In his film, Vice President Gore used graphic demonstrations of the scientific evidence behind the growth in carbon emissions, and their climate change impact. Since his cinematic debut, the vice president's thesis—that "greenhouse-effect" climate change is caused by increased carbon emissions from human sources—won broad-based acceptance from the scientific community.

Government Response to Climate Change

The 2004 Kyoto Protocol was the international response to climate change. But the U.S., the world's largest emitter of greenhouse gases, failed to sign the Protocol. President George W. Bush was fundamentally opposed to any regulation on carbon on the basis that it disproportionately harmed large economies such as the U.S. And while Protocol signers such as the UK, France, and Japan soldiered on to fight climate change with their own regulatory regimes, America had orphaned their efforts.

But on April 17, 2009, that all changed. On that date, President Obama's U.S. Environmental Protection Agency head Lisa Jackson declared climate change a public safety hazard, allowing the EPA to start to impose greenhouse gas (GHG) emission limits under the authority of the existing Clean Air and Clean Water Acts. The EPA ruling effectively ended more than a decade of American official neutrality in the war on climate change. The EPA ruling was nothing less than the climate change equivalent of the U.S. government's unprecedented activist role in remediating the 2008–2009 debt crisis.

The EPA ruling cleared the way for lawmakers in the U.S. Congress to create a cap-and-trade market for carbon emissions. While a carbon tax or government-mandated carbon sequestration programs (such as those being readied by China) are also potentially viable alternative climate change measures, market-based cap-and-trade solutions have far fewer negative political impacts than a tax. Many Obama administration officials, including the president's energy and environment "czarina" Carol Browner (who served as EPA administrator under President Clinton) remember the electoral backlash against Democratic President Clinton's 1993 attempt to impose a tax on energy generators based on their BTU (British Thermal Units, the standard measure for generation of heat) outputs. Many credit the BTU tax backlash with causing 1994's "Republican Revolution," which resulted in Republican majorities in both the U.S. House and U.S. Senate, creating legislative gridlock for the last six years of President Clinton's eight years in office. Because the proposed BTU tax had such a high political cost, we believe that any regime other than a market-based cap-and-trade system is dead on arrival.

In a cap-and-trade system, the U.S. has several viable models from which to choose. Chief among them are the UN Framework Convention on Climate Change (UNFCCC) model, the European Union Emission Trading Scheme, and the now-voluntary Chicago Climate Exchange. In any of these systems, a price for a ton of carbon emissions will be set, either by the government or by the market. All trading counterparties will need good accounting and oversight to establish fair value and a cost basis for carbon. And within a short period of time, the costs associated with carbon emissions will make those whose processes are most carbon-efficient the most cost-competitive.

We see The Post-Carbon Economy as the result of several recent historic threads. Globalization and the rise of America's service economy made the world wealthier; populations grew, fossil fuel use increased, carbon emissions rose, climates started changing and altering the economic landscape. Financial engineering accelerated the growth of the service economy, creating a debt bubble that burst tragically in 2008, forcing governments from the United States to UK to Germany to Belgium to Japan to China to step in to save financial markets. The economic crash accelerated U.S. private sector and public sector structural change away from overwhelmingly service economy-driven to a more balanced post-carbon model. In the service economy of the 1990s, carbon emissions and waste represented virtually zero cost and therefore, carbon and waste efficiency gave proponents no competitive advantage. In The Post-Carbon Economy, nonproductive outputs such as GHG

Exhibit 3

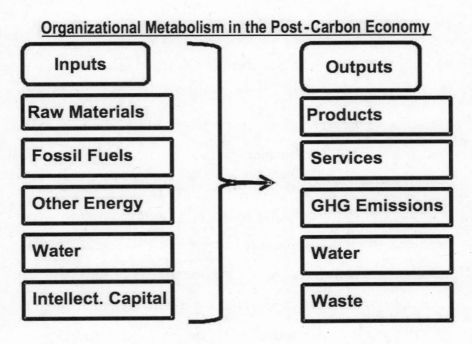

Organizational Metabolism in the Post-Carbon Economy

Inputs	Outputs
Raw Materials	Products
Fossil Fuels	Services
Other Energy	GHG Emissions
Water	Water
Intellect. Capital	Waste

© 2009 by Amit Chatterjee and Jay Whitehead

emissions and waste are associated with significant costs, and regardless of labor cost advantages, wasteful practices result in a competitive disadvantage. We call this condition an imbalance in an organization's metabolism. Because in The Post-Carbon Economy these nonproductive outputs actually do represent waste and involve significant costs, organizational sustainability means accounting for the nonproductive output costs and managing to reduce them.

By early summer 2009, The Post-Carbon Economy was already taking shape. The 2008–2009 debt crisis caused some hard-pressed companies to make post-carbon alterations in their businesses—cut business travel, cut high-carbon energy generation plants for lack of capital market support, re-engineer processes for minimum waste. For the rest, governmental regulatory response to climate change made structural change inevitable. And just as the U.S. government's debt-crisis re-regulation of financial markets changed the cost of financing everything, new government-imposed costs on carbon emissions will impact the cost of nearly all products and services. The Post-Carbon Economy will change your company, country, and career in ways happy and harsh. Yet the more you understand it, the more you can turn your understanding of The Post-Carbon Economy into your own personal recession-avoidance strategy. Getting ahead of the carbon curve will be, for many, the biggest business opportunity of all time.

Chapter 2

If You Only Ever Read One Thing about Climate Change, Read This Chapter. A Layman's Guide to Carbon-Based Climate Change: Where's the Heat, Who Makes It, How to Control It, and Where's the Money?

Meet Carbon, Global Warming's Heat Source, and the Men (and Women) Who Made It Infamous

Vice President Al Gore, with his 2007 Academy Award-winning documentary film and paperback best-seller *An Inconvenient Truth*, elevated climate change from conference chatter to cause célèbre. On his Web site, the vice president eloquently describes the science and implications of global warming:

Carbon dioxide and other gases warm the surface of the planet naturally by trapping solar heat in the atmosphere. This is a good thing because it keeps our planet habitable. However, by burning fossil fuels such as coal, gas and oil and clearing forests we have dramatically increased the amount of carbon dioxide in the Earth's atmosphere and temperatures are rising.

The vast majority of scientists agree that global warming is real, it's already happening and that it is the result of our activities and not a natural occurrence. The evidence is overwhelming and undeniable.... If the warming continues, we can expect catastrophic consequences. Deaths from global warming will double in just 25 years—to 300,000 people a year. Global sea levels could rise by more than 20 feet with the loss of shelf ice in Greenland and Antarctica, devastating coastal areas worldwide. Heat waves will be more frequent and more intense. Droughts and wildfires will occur more often. The Arctic Ocean could be ice free in summer by 2050. More than a million species worldwide could be driven to extinction by 2050.[4]

An Inconvenient Truth achieved the unexpected by catalyzing environmental activism among governments, companies, nonprofit groups and individuals worldwide. For his work, the former vice president shared the Nobel Peace Prize with the UN's Intergovernmental Panel on Climate Change, which endorsed his thesis that humans are causing the warming.

In his cinematic explanation of the accelerating impact of the "greenhouse effect," the vice president cited the U.S. Environmental Protection Agency (EPA) estimate that 85 percent of all greenhouse gas (GHG) emissions are carbon dioxide, or CO_2. This is why science uses CO_2e, or carbon dioxide equivalents, to measure all emissions. That's how, despite the presence of other regional GHGs such as sulfur dioxide (SO_2), nitrogen oxide (NOX) and Mercury, carbon has become the focus of all anti-climate change activity. And that's why accounting for carbon is the topic of this book.

After telling the climate change story more than 1,000 times over 10 years to a total audience of nearly 1 billion, Al Gore certainly earned his Oscar and Nobel accolades. But the climate research scientist whose work first sounded the carbon dioxide alarm is much less famous. Dr. Charles David Keeling of the Scripps Institute of Oceanography, whose "Keeling Curve" dates back to 1958, toiled in near-anonymity, yet his work remains to this day the most important science in global warming. Dr. Keeling's pioneering carbon level measurements from his station in Mauna Loa, Hawaii, showed an alarming rise in carbon dioxide levels, from 315 parts per million (ppm) in the atmosphere in 1958 to 380 ppm in 2005.

Exhibit 4

The Keeling Curve, Atmospheric Carbon Dioxide Levels 1959–2005

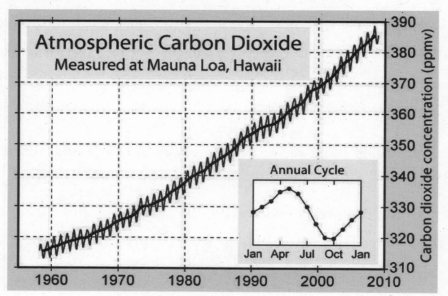

The Keeling Curve's vegetation-based seasonal variations in CO2 levels led Princeton physicist Freeman Dyson to his 1976 suggestion of a "carbon bank" of fast-growing trees to cut atmospheric carbon content.

The Keeling Curve was the first science-based greenhouse effect warning, and despite losing his funding in his study's fourth year, Keeling's work finally achieved official recognition in 1965 from President Johnson's Science Advisory Committee report. In 1976 the Princeton physicist Freeman Dyson, noting the squiggly line seasonal variation in Keeling Curve measurements and attributing them to carbon releasing and absorbing qualities of Hawaiian vegetation, wrote a seminal paper "Can We Control the Carbon Dioxide in the Atmosphere?" In his work, Dyson proposed the idea of a "carbon bank" of fast-growing trees. Dyson's work was among several that suggested the practicality and even the commercial potential of capturing carbon emissions using photosynthetic and other types of carbon sequestration. Today, dozens of sequestration solutions are being actively pursued by governments, energy companies, and public-private partnerships, primary among them capturing and storing CO_2 underground (known as geological storage, or GS) and in natural carbon-absorbing "sinks" of trees and other agricultural crops. And all these advances started with Keeling's Curve.

Keeling's work was seminal. Yet it is one thing to measure atmospheric carbon, and quite another to get companies to count their emissions. This was the task faced by the Carbon Disclosure Project (CDP), a British nonprofit that back in 2003 came up with a diabolically simple way to pressure companies to count their carbon: Get their investors to make them do it. So the CDP, powered by funding from Merrill Lynch and a strong cast of international political and media leaders including German Prime Minister Angela Merkel, former President Clinton, and Newscorp Chairman Rupert Murdoch, was able to gather 385 institutional investor signatories representing a combined asset base of $57 trillion. And by the 2008 reporting cycle, the sixth in the series, 321, or 64 percent of Standard & Poors 500 companies had participated, with more expected for 2009. The CDP database is a classic example of the business mantra "what gets measured, gets managed." What's more, its creation has arguably been the single-greatest accelerator of voluntary company emission improvements as well as market-based and regulation-based initiatives to cut CO2e.

The first suggestion of a "cap-and-trade" approach to carbon came in 1970 from National Air Pollution Control Administration officials Ellison Burton and William Sanjour, whose mathematical models found a "least cost solution" for any level of air pollution abatement. Those models led to "offset mechanisms" used in 1977's Clean Air Act and a rudimentary cap-and-trade program launched in 1988 as part of the U.S. Acid Rain Program. Following the limited success of the acid rain trading effort involving the U.S. and Canada, the potential of a global climate policy emerged. The British adapted the success to their market and created the UK Emissions Trading Scheme in 1999, resulting in the first semi-commercial market for carbon credits. Based on the UK success, a similar regime was adopted starting in February 2005 by the European Union as the EU Emission Trading Scheme (EU ETS). By early 2009, the EU ETS covered more than 10,000 installations in the energy and industrial sectors representing 50 percent of the EU's CO2 emissions and 40 percent of all its GHG emissions. Under the EU ETS, EU member states agree on national caps that are approved by the EU commission and allocated to industrial operators. At year end, the allowances are retired by trading with other operators privately, via spot markets or through brokers. The trades work just like a stock market, with traders agreeing on a price and settling by exchanging value.

While market-based "cap-and-trade" models have experienced success in remediating CO2e, trying to reach the same goal by taxing energy users has led to some notable failures. President Bill Clinton tried unsuccessfully to slap on a BTU (British Thermal Units, a measure of heat output) tax, which would have immediately hiked utility prices, penalizing consumers. For the Clinton administration, that resulted in a political disaster that many pundits believe helped the Republican Party take over Congress in 1994, stifling many of Democratic President Clinton's initiatives. Several Clinton administration officials with first-hand memories of this harsh lesson moved into the Obama White House. Most notable among them Carol Browner, Clinton's EPA administrator, and Obama's "czarina" for energy and climate. As a result, in 2009, "cap-and-trade" finally got friends in high places.

So with CDP participation accelerating and a new carbon-focused government in place, the American business and political stage was set. And with the political will, the money followed. The first months of the Obama administration and new Democratic Congress delivered $40 billion in renewable energy grants and loans, $11 billion for solar and wind power electricity lines, and $75 billion in green energy R&D tax cuts. Fortunately, just as the money came, the science was ready, with new technologies for energy efficiency, low-emission energy generation, CO2 sequestration and carbon off-setting in place, and many more in development. And despite the momentarily low energy prices of early 2009, markets for carbon trading were also set, having gained large-scale experience and customers in Europe and in the voluntary markets in the U.S. and Canada.

Yet the entire post-carbon scene was not complete. There was at least one group of cast members still necessary to provide business leaders with the confidence to undertake large-scale cap-and-trade activities: insurance actuaries. They finally joined the show in mid-March 2009. That's when the National

Association of Insurance Commissioners ruled insurance companies must submit annual "climate-risk" reports. The insurers reached their pronouncement after actuaries were able to plot the real probabilities of climate change-driven extreme weather, floods, and wildfires boosting claims. In addition, insurance executives realized that once their actuaries had spoken, governments would have a basis upon which to cap industrial carbon emissions that contribute to global warming—a move that could impact the profitability of coal-fueled utilities in which insurers often invest.

With the president, Congress, the EPA, and hundreds of business leaders including the all-important insurance commissioners, the scene was now set for a U.S. government-mandated cap-and-trade-based system of carbon emission reduction processes to start. In its earliest phases, the cap-and-trade programs will pit profit-hungry traders against derivative securities-weary and cost-sensitive companies, creating sparks. As the trading markets mature and more companies understand the securities, a steady state will emerge and carbon emission growth will measurably slow. Then as energy-saving and low-emission technologies become cheaper than coal and oil, more advanced companies will shed their dependence on the carbon trading markets, while companies with older and more emission-producing power generating capabilities will remain dependent on the carbon credit markets indefinitely, until all the affordable oil and coal are burned up.

For the purposes of this book, the specific carbon-limiting mechanism is less important than the fact that a price gets set. Whether America's ultimate cap-and-trade system for carbon credits mirrors the UN Framework Convention on Climate Change (UNFCCC), the EU-ETS, or the Chicago Climate Exchange, or whether governments auction promises to buy a stream of emissions rather than relying 100 percent on company counterparties for trades is but a detail. This book is primarily concerned with one eventuality: Any trading scheme sets a price on a ton of CO2e. Once there is a price for CO2e, carbon becomes a cost included in every product and service we buy and sell and use. And that is the fundamental definition of The Post-Carbon Economy.

Meet the Businesses Making Heat

In the U.S. in 2009, the most CO2e-intensive activities involve electricity generation and transportation. Electric utilities represent 41 percent of emissions, while transportation makes up 34 percent. Building, manufacturing, meat production, other business and human activities and natural phenomena produce the remaining 25 percent.

The greatest achievement of the Carbon Disclosure Project (other than the genius and miracle of its mere existence) is in revealing where businesses' greatest opportunities for CO2e remediation lie. A side-by-side comparison of company CO2e levels shows that America's electric utilities are by far the largest emitters in gross CO2e tonnage. But more important than a company's CO2e gross tons is a measure we call the Carbon Impact Ratio, defined as a company's CO2e in tons divided by the company's revenue. (The CDP calls this ratio "intensity," a term we find less than ideally descriptive and action oriented than our term Carbon Impact Ratio.)

Exhibit 5

S&P 500 Companies with Greatest Opportunity per Revenue Dollar to Cut Carbon Emissions
Company Carbon Impact Ratios--Carbon Dioxide Equivalents (CO2e) Divided by Revenues
Industries Ranked by Greatest Opportunity to Reduce Carbon

Industry	Company	Carbon Impact Ratio (CO2e/Revenues)	CO2e (tons)
Utilities	American Electric Power	11,682	156,300,000
	Dynegy	10,363	32,900,000
	Southern Company	9,835	151,000,000
	Ameren Corporation	9,036	68,188,741
	Duke Energy	8,145	103,600,000
	Dominion Resources	7,477	117,188,199
	Xcel Energy	6,036	60,567,132
	Progress Energy	5,797	53,062,972
	PPL Corporation	4,832	31,400,000
	FPL Group	4,350	68,346,000
	Entergy	2,931	33,658,088
	PSEG	2,009	25,827,743
	XTO Energy	926	5,103,119
	Exelon Corporation	589	11,150,000
	Consolidated Edison	493	6,467,230
	PG&E	178	2,353,152

Exhibit 5 (cont'd)

S&P 500 Companies with Greatest Opportunity per Revenue Dollar to Cut Carbon Emissions			
Company Carbon Impact Ratios–Carbon Dioxide Equivalents (CO2e) Divided by Revenues			
Industries Ranked by Greatest Opportunity to Reduce Carbon			
Industry	Company	Carbon Impact Ratio (CO2e/Revenues)	CO2e (tons)
Oil & Gas	El Paso Corporation	3,354	15,590,990
	Williams Companies	1,680	17,740,000
	Occidental Petroleum	841	15,900,000
	Exxon Mobil	589	137,000,000
	Conoco Phillips	328	63,706,198
	Chevron	275	60,661,935
	Hess Corporation	202	6,395,439
Raw Materials, Mining, Paper & Packaging	US Steel	2,865	48,341,091
	Alcoa	1,919	59,000,000
	Weyerhauser	460	7,500,000
	Plum Creek Timber	21	35,149
Chemicals/Pharmaceuticals	Air Products	2,192	22,000,000
	Praxair	1,507	14,168,433
	Dow	691	37,300,000
	PPG	618	6,927,127
	DuPont	476	14,000,000
	Abbott	66	1,704,256
	Baxter International	65	727,790
	Bristol Myers-Squibb	50	972,299
	Pfizer	45	2,194,173
	Schering-Plough	44	558,349
	Allergan	30	118,753
	Johnson & Johnson	15	923,151

Exhibit 5 (cont'd)

S&P 500 Companies with Greatest Opportunity per Revenue Dollar to Cut Carbon Emissions
Company Carbon Impact Ratios--Carbon Dioxide Equivalents (CO2e) Divided by Revenues
Industries Ranked by Greatest Opportunity to Reduce Carbon

Industry	Company	Carbon Impact Ratio (CO2e/Revenues)	CO2e (tons)
Transportation	Burlington Northern	947	14,964,923
	CSX	653	6,529,067
	UPS	167	8,243,743
Leisure & Lodging	Carnival	763	9,940,270
	Marriott	229	2,982,878
	Simon Property	220	802,941
	ProLogis	1	9,220
Retail & Consumer	Kimberly-Clark	340	6,201,391
	Coca-Cola Company	173	4,920,000
	Molson Coors	151	1,254,563
	Pepsico	96	3,802,514
	HJ Heinz	91	911,395
	Procter & Gamble	83	6,347,000
	Sara Lee Corporation	71	871,608
	Brown-Forman	65	168,856
	Wal-Mart	54	20,240,815
	Colgate-Palmolive	49	675,076
	Target	45	2,874,017
	Gap	43	674,377
	Starbucks	31	295,000

Exhibit 5 (cont'd)

S&P 500 Companies with Greatest Opportunity per Revenue Dollar to Cut Carbon Emissions

Company Carbon Impact Ratios--Carbon Dioxide Equivalents (CO2e) Divided by Revenues

Industries Ranked by Greatest Opportunity to Reduce Carbon

Industry	Company	Carbon Impact Ratio (CO2e/Revenues)	CO2e (tons)
Heavy Manufacturing	3M	372	9,090,000
	Eaton	73	949,000
	Cummins	64	833,049
	Deere	58	1,390,402
	GM	53	9,590,000
	Caterpillar	52	2,348,000
	Ford	33	5,761,631
	Boeing	25	1,692,000
Technology & Business Services	Eastman Kodak	184	1,892,108
	Verizon	81	7,550,076
	Johnson Controls	48	1,656,977
	Raytheon	31	661,930
	IBM	29	2,865,118
	Xerox	23	394,909
	EMC Corporation	20	263,883
	Pitney Bowes	17	101,792
	Cisco	16	545,173
	HP	15	1,518,107
	Juniper Networks	13	38,255
	Motorola	10	375,328
	Dell Inc.	7	438,338
	AT&T	5	622,226
	Microsoft	3	167,580

Exhibit 5 (cont'd)

S&P 500 Companies with Greatest Opportunity per Revenue Dollar to Cut Carbon Emissions			
Company Carbon Impact Ratios--Carbon Dioxide Equivalents (CO2e) Divided by Revenues			
Industries Ranked by Greatest Opportunity to Reduce Carbon			
Industry	Company	Carbon Impact Ratio (CO2e/Revenues)	CO2e (tons)
Financial Services	Citigroup	17	1,411,481
	Comerica	13	62,029
	Bank of America	12	1,422,791
	Allstate	8	278,655
	Franklin Resources	5	29,370
	Hartford Financial	5	144,011
	Legg Mason	4	18,503
	Travelers Companies	3	73,679
	Genworth Financial	2	16,830

Source: Carbon Disclosure Project 2008 Report on S&P 500 (47% responding)

By comparing peer companies in a given industry sector, the Carbon Impact Ratio shows which companies are efficient and which have the largest opportunities to find efficiencies. For example, compare American Electric Power's Carbon Impact Ratio (11,682) with PG&E's (178). For every dollar of its revenues, PG&E emits 65 times (11682/178 = 65.63) less CO2e than AEP. This points out how the Carbon Impact Ratio can help competitors in the same industry improve quickly. The lowest hanging fruit in terms of intra-industry competitive advantage is for those with high Carbon Impact Ratios to emulate those with the lowest. By copying PG&E, AEP can save itself potentially many billions of dollars in carbon costs.

Meet Climate Change's Kryptonite—or—How "Carbon Efficiency" is Your Key to Competitive Advantage in *The Post-Carbon Economy*

Despite all indications that we are already in The Post-Carbon Economy, we have recently read opinion pieces in major periodicals claiming that climate change is any or all of the following:

- a conspiracy theory concocted by environmentalists and Hollywood to extort contributions from donors and sell movie tickets,

- impossible for American business to impact because the emissions from fast-growing economies such as China will overwhelm any reductions in the U.S.,

- a natural cycle that will not impact humans or environmental conditions.

For the record, we know all of these writers are misinformed. What the science shows is that if or when atmospheric CO_2e rises from its 2009 level of 390 parts per million by volume to 500 ppmv, we will have reached the so-called 2-degree Celcius threshold, resulting in an environmental disaster that will raise sea levels 15 feet, turn major agricultural regions such as the American Midwest and South and southern Europe into deserts. The economic impact of this climate change would be to drop U.S. gross domestic product by one-third and result in the death by hunger, heat, or flood of up to 1 billion people worldwide.

So as far as we are concerned, the climate change debate is over. At this point, losing time in arguing with uninformed climate change skeptics makes remediating CO2e much more difficult—and costs you the chance to build a large competitive advantage in The Post-Carbon Economy. Putting it a different way, if you just discovered critical new information that would allow you to build a substantial lead over your competitors, would you waste any time in pursuing that advantage? Our bet is that you would immediately seize the new info and use it to beat your rival.

That is what The Post-Carbon Economy is. It is critical new information for you to use against your commercial adversaries. In comic books, the antidote to Superman's super powers was Kryptonite. In The Post-Carbon Economy, your version of Kryptonite for climate change is what we call "carbon efficiency."

"Carbon efficiency" is a simple concept: the most carbon efficient companies emit the smallest net amount of CO2e per unit of production among their peers. It may be a simple concept, but carbon efficiency is made complex by the nature of CO2e emissions—they nearly all come from energy sources in thousands of different places throughout our businesses. Therein lies the challenge. All the value in our businesses depends on energy. While we cannot create value without energy inputs, most energy comes from CO2e-emitting sources. So how can we become carbon efficient if CO2e seems to be a necessary output from most economic activity?

The truth is that while energy is a required input, net CO2e emissions are not necessary outputs. CO2e outputs can be gobbled up by "carbon sinks," typically agricultural assets such as trees or grass fields that consume CO2 as part of their photosynthetic processes. Thousands of producers have created certified "offsets" from these sinks, which are now being bought and sold on exchanges such as the Chicago Climate Exchange. CO2e outputs can be eliminated or replaced by using non-CO2e-emitting energy sources such as wind- or solar-generated electricity. They can be reduced using energy-conservation techniques such as enhanced insulation. Or they can be sequestered, which involves warehousing the emissions by piping them into, for example, porous portions of the Earth's crust.

In the past decade, a cottage industry of carbon efficiency advisors has sprouted up. The state-of-the-art in carbon advisory services boils down to charting, comparing, and cost-mapping your CO2e emissions and identifying remediation paths that minimize costs.

A classic first step taken by advisors is to chart a distribution of an enterprise's GHG assets along with its corresponding remediation/reduction targets. On the following page is a typical pie chart of CO2e emissions from a small electric utility, along with the reduction targets and recommended remediation methods.

As the pie chart on the following page shows, carbon efficiency means employing many tools toward one objective: minimizing your business' net outputs of CO2e from its inputs of energy. Carbon efficiency, however, is not something that businesses will pursue without first considering costs.

While the pie chart is a worthwhile tool used by leading carbon management advisory firms, another way to look at carbon efficiency costs is to map your opportunities and rank them according to their estimated cost reductions or increases. While a CO2e reduction opportunity map for an electric utility as shown on the next page will differ significantly from that of other businesses, it gives you an idea of some of the relative estimated costs of some of the major types of CO2e reduction actions you can take. In this example, biodiesel costs 44 percent more than current fuel sources, and improved insulation can save nearly 150 percent over current energy uses.

Exhibit 6

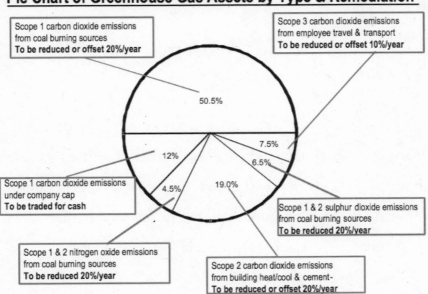

Pie Chart of Greenhouse Gas Assets by Type & Remediation

Scope 1 carbon dioxide emissions from coal burning sources **To be reduced or offset 20%/year**

Scope 3 carbon dioxide emissions from employee travel & transport **To be reduced or offset 10%/year**

50.5%

7.5%

12%

6.5%

4.5%

19.0%

Scope 1 carbon dioxide emissions under company cap **To be traded for cash**

Scope 1 & 2 sulphur dioxide emissions from coal burning sources **To be reduced 20%/year**

Scope 1 & 2 nitrogen oxide emissions from coal burning sources **To be reduced 20%/year**

Scope 2 carbon dioxide emissions from building heat/cool & cement- **To be reduced or offset 20%/year**

Exhibit 7

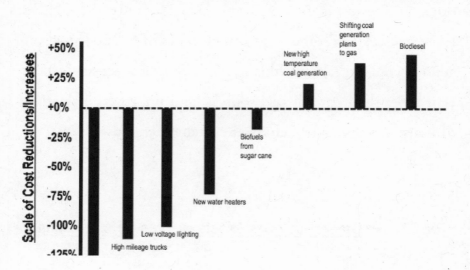

Mapping CO2e Reduction Opportunities by Cost

© 2009 by Jay Whitehead and Amit Chatterjee. Cost estimates based on U.S. EPA and U.S. Department of Energy data.

Many businesses have choices over the fuels they use for energy inputs. It is likely that you already know your costs per unit of the fuels that your business uses. But few companies understand the CO2e emissions of each, compared with the other optional replacement fuels.

Exhibit 8

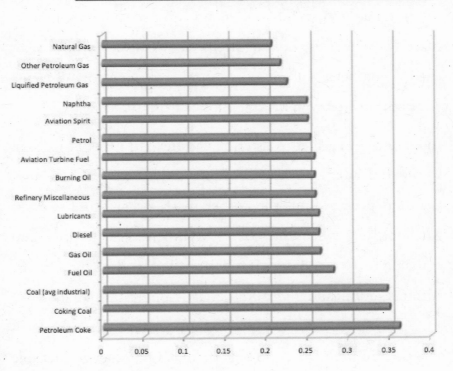

CO2e Emissions by Common Fuel Type

■ kg CO2 per KWI
Source: Swivel.com

The chart on above showing the CO2e emissions by common fuel type will help get you oriented. Among the fuels on the chart, natural gas emits the least, while coal emits 76 percent more CO2e per kilowatt hour (kWh).

So let's assume that at this point in your journey to carbon efficiency you know your overall CO2e emissions outputs and understand the costs for your energy inputs. Knowing another piece of the cost puzzle, the pricing signals from carbon credit trading markets, will give you another avenue for offsetting your outputs, or even making money from them.

In chapter 6, entitled Mastering the Ins and Outs of Carbon Cap-and-Trade, we take a dive into the existing carbon markets and peek around the corner to see what those markets will look like when the U.S. government sets its price and emission level mandates. The bottom line is this: the Obama administration and the 2009–2010 Congress have shown a strong preference for a cap-and-trade system that sets both a legal minimum price for a ton of CO2e and enforceable emission caps for each company. Once that happens, your business will know for certain what price you can ask for your carbon credits (if you emit less than your allotted amount or own agricultural assets that act as certified carbon sinks to offset CO2e emissions) or must pay for your emissions.

The theory behind carbon cap-and-trade is to use market forces to reduce emissions while generating revenues that will be used to remediate climate change. Because the U.S. government has already used cap-and-trade successfully in its acid rain reduction program for electric utilities, it has confidence that the program will affordably improve the environment.

While cap-and-trade costs will get most attention because they mimic a tax on carbon emissions, it is just one of the major cost and emission variables on your path to competitive advantage through carbon efficiency. The others are: comparative CO2e emissions of fossil fuels and renewable, fossil fuel energy costs from existing sources; technological improvements in energy generation and conservation; and government and other incentives to adopt the improvements. The image on the next page captures four trend lines that represent the variables.

Using the chart on the following page, your post-carbon objective is to get your business on one or more of the descending lines while minimizing your exposure to the ascending line.

Exhibit 9

Combining Cap-and-Trade, Energy Price Hikes, New-Tech Generation & Conservation, and Incentives to Drive Competitive Advantage through Carbon Efficiency

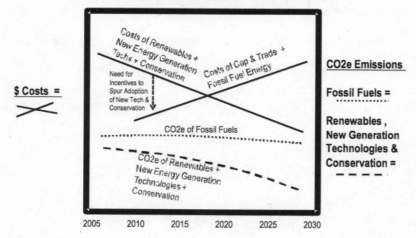

© 2009 by Amit Chatterjee and Jay Whitehead

In energy prices, oil and gas billionaire and wind power investor T. Boone Pickens told Jay Whitehead at the CRO Summit event in Chicago in October 2008, "Fossil fuel energy prices will inevitably go up. It's basic supply-and-demand, and while there are plenty of oil and gas reserves, they are continuously more expensive to drill and refine and deliver. Any dips in fossil fuel prices are strictly temporary." Continuously more expensive fossil fuels create incentives for innovation in alternative energy sources.

As oil prices hit the historic high levels above $100 per barrel rate in late 2007 and early 2008, the founders of Google conceived their Renewable Energy Less Expensive than Coal, or RE<C initiative, a research and development effort inspired by higher energy costs. RE<C was just one of hundreds of such investment programs to create affordable alternative energy sources. From January 2004 to April 2009, *CRO* magazine reported that over $83 billion in alternative energy research and development corporate and venture capital investments have poured into alternative and renewable energy technologies. To be cost-competitive, nearly all of them count on either or both of two factors: higher fossil fuel prices, or government incentives. As a result of both higher traditional fuel prices and government incentives, you will see a proliferation of affordable low CO_2e-emitting renewable sources, offering businesses more choices for building a carbon efficiency competitive advantage. Our prediction is that early adopters of the new energy sources will gain the greatest edge. And those who choose the energy sources with the lowest CO_2e emissions profile will gain the greatest edge.

In energy generation and conservation technologies, recent developments have delivered a stunning array of new offerings. This proliferation of choices and rapid cascades of innovation both will deliver cost and CO2e reductions, and will continue to make investment decisions tougher. Fear of missing the newest thing or of betting on a dead-end technology will freeze some companies in their tracks. As a result of both buyers' fears and significant capital costs or cost premiums from the new technologies, government incentives will be very important to get business uptake. In China, government support for new coal-burning technologies such as the high-temperature CCS plants will be required to keep that fast-growing economy from overwhelming the world's atmosphere carbon emissions. Back here in the U.S., in the first quarter of 2009 for example, the U.S. government invested $6 billion in a program to insulate residences in major metropolitan areas at government expense. This program will represent energy savings that never would be realized outside of the presence of a subsidy.

Your company's post-carbon competitive advantage lies in employing a combination of cost and emission savings that both makes you the lowest net-emitting competitor, but also the lowest net-cost. We are certain that your competitive advantage in The Post-Carbon Economy will involve a cocktail of the "5 I's": incentives, innovations, investments, insulation, and ingenuity. Which "I's" you will use, and the combination in which you use them will involve an artful balance, and will require regular adjustment throughout all your business processes.

Chapter 3

The 5 Secrets to Success in The Post-Carbon Economy

When we set out to write *The Post-Carbon Economy* in early 2009, we thought our biggest obstacle (after sleep deprivation) would be the distraction of the then-current economic crisis. When the economy is racking up more than 600,000 jobless claims a month, we thought, who focuses on carbon? But we met with a big surprise. The recession, as it turns out, accelerated many companies, industries, and governments into Post-Carbon Economy thinking. Necessity had already been the mother of many Post-Carbon Economy inventions.

Crushed by record falling demand and unprecedented cost pressures from competitors, customers, and capital markets, thousands of companies in dozens of industries adopted Post-Carbon Economy-type innovations. The list of examples is long and getting longer. Their innovations in the face of cost pressures gave hints of the shape of the Post-Carbon Economy.

Start with the carbon-intensive industries. Utilities (UTX, Duke Energy) have been forced by capital markets to scrap plans for expensive old-style coal-fired power plants in favor of newer, cleaner, financing-friendly technologies. Cement companies, whose products and processes are responsible for 5 percent of human-caused CO_2, are now creating formulations to be a form of CO_2 sequestration (examples include Cemstone's products in the making of Minneapolis' new St. Anthony Falls Bridge). Energy firms (BP, Exxon), despite momentary low prices for oil and gas and near-record profits from their carbon-based sources, continue to invest at least $10 billion annually in clean technologies as the source of future competitive advantage (although this investment dwarfs the $369 billion spent globally on oil exploration).

The besieged automotive sector (most notably Ford, GM, Toyota, and Honda) has turned to non-carbon-fuel-based propulsion as its only way back to eventual profitability. Carmakers in the U.S. (GM, Ford), Japan (Toyota, Honda), India (Tata Motors), and France (Renault) are preparing actively for the coming era of the electric car, addressing engineering challenges (including CEO Shai Agassi's Better replacement battery scheme, plug-in rechargeable and internal generator models), and psychological barriers such as driver "range anxiety."

In the building trades, energy-conserving technologies and cradle-to-cradle sustainable manufacturing techniques are helping keep building outfitters (Interface) in business and insulation makers (Dow, Monsanto) profitable. In travel, while there is still no viable substitute for carbon-based jet fuel, the International Air Transport Association cut out purchase of paper tickets, saving $9 per flight, and even a little bit of carbon.[5] Forest products companies are turning from logging to wood waste-based alternative energy production and to creating new revenue sources in tradable carbon-offset credits.[6]

Manufacturers from packaged goods (examples include Seventh Generation, Procter & Gamble) to office furniture (Herman Miller) to industrial floor coverings (Interface) to tractors (Caterpillar) have turned to closed-cycle manufacturing, which turns old products into the raw materials for new products, building sustainable supply chains and lowering carbon footprints along the way. High technology companies (Intel, TI, Fairchild, National, AMD, IBM, Cypress, Sunpower) are finding new boom niches in low-emission energy-saving product lines. Retailers (Wal-Mart, IKEA) are driving radical reductions in packaging size, shipping costs, and usage of plastic bags, paper bags, and energy.

The list goes on. Despite the collapse of the IPO markets, venture capital firms (Kleiner Perkins, Khosla, Sequoia, and hundreds of others) continue to invest many billions of dollars in post-carbon economy business models. Professional service businesses (PWC, Deloitte, Accenture, Grant Thornton), are morphing their business models to actively avoid carbon emission-intensive business travel, with PWC in btnonline.com reporting a recent 79 percent increase in virtual meetings on March 30, 2009. While two data points do not make a trend, dozens do.

While companies make post-carbon-type changes themselves to cut costs during the 2008–2009 recession, history shows that once economic growth returns, spending habits tend to follow. But the new reality of The Post-Carbon Economy is that once an effective U.S. government price has been set on a ton of CO2e, the new level of costs involved in remediating carbon emissions will forever change the economics of many sectors, making reversion to 2006-style "business spending as usual" impossible.

Chapter 4

Secret 1: The Carbon Efficiency Challenge: Keep Growing While Pursuing NZI

The first secret to success of The Post-Carbon Economy is that while cutting greenhouse gas production, your business and the economy have to continue to grow. Not a simple outcome to achieve. Not simple, especially considering this: Given a choice between stemming climate change in the future and making immediate economic sacrifice, all recent opinion polls have shown that Americans want to go carbon neutral, but are unwilling to take any voluntary personal financial hits to get there. As CEO Stephen Joyce of the 5,800-unit lodging giant Choice Hotels told us, "Consumers like staying at so-called green hotels, but woe unto you if you ask them to pay extra for the privilege or tell them they can't have something for the sake of its giant carbon footprint."

Multiple studies, most notably Resources for the Future's November 2008 discussion paper "Impact of Carbon Price Policies on U.S. Industry," shows that a unilateral economy-wide $10/ton CO2e charge causes dramatic changes in short-term costs, capital allocations, outputs, exports, and employment, although adverse impacts on profits diminish rapidly in a couple years. While $10/ton is a low-end estimate of the effective CO2e price set by the a U.S. government (McKinsey says it's more like $50/ton, and many industries will actually benefit from carbon cuts in the long-term, business leaders are understandably most worried about the immediate-term impact of The Post-Carbon Economy.[7]

How do we bridge the gap? How to avoid climate change while keeping the economy growing? Let's start to answer the question by looking at the math of manmade climate change.

First, what is the maximum level of carbon emission equivalents, or CO2e the atmosphere can stand before climate change becomes so drastic that it will have significant economic impact?

Nicholas Stern, in his seminal 2006 paper "The Economics of Climate Change" suggested that to stabilize the climate, humans would by 2050 need to reduce CO2e emissions by 76 percent from 2008 levels.[8]

To get a little more granular about that number, let's look at the maximum level of atmospheric carbon dioxide (in parts per million by volume, or CO2e ppmv) the science community has concluded it is necessary to stay under to avoid permanent climate change damage to the world economy. That consensus maximum CO2e ppmv level is 500 ppmv. As of early 2009, the level measured at Mauna Loa, Hawaii, was 390 and rising… rapidly. In the past 35 years, the measured atmospheric CO2e level has risen 20 percent. Another 11 percent, and we're at the threshold. And keep in mind, the world population in 2010 at 6.3 billion is 18 percent larger than 1975, and the 2010 world economy is nearly 40 percent larger than in 1975. Time to act.

So let's assume that 500 ppmv is the maximum CO2e level the atmosphere can handle without global warming doing great economic damage. That means that we assume that once the CO2e level gets above 500, the climate change impact on agriculture and habitability of population centers will be so negative that great worldwide financial disruption is a certainty. As we said earlier, some will argue with this point. But our job here is not to debate global warming impacts. Our job is to show you how to succeed in The Post-Carbon Economy. So let's keep going.

Assuming no new technological advances in clean energy, how much is it going to cost to keep us from hitting the 500 ppmv maximum target? Thankfully, the McKinsey Global Institute's blockbuster June 2008 report, "The Carbon Productivity Challenge: Curbing Climate Change and Sustaining Economic Growth," gave us the world's first credible macroeconomic estimates of the price of climate change abatement.[9]

The McKinsey report shows that to meet the 2050 carbon emission target of keeping CO2e ppmv levels under 500, each business must increase its "carbon efficiency" by a factor of ten, from \$740 in Gross Domestic Product per ton of CO_2e produced in 2009 to \$7,300 by 2050. The McKinsey report authors note that this scale of transformation is analogous to executing the economic transformation involved in the 120 years of the Industrial Revolution in one-third the time— 40 years. (Authors' Note: Throughout this book, we use the term "carbon efficiency" because most business people understand the everyday reality of being efficient in their processes. McKinsey uses the term "carbon productivity," which refers to macroeconomic impact.)

Going to the next step, McKinsey worked with The Vattenfall Institute of Economic Research to identify the lowest-cost sources of the estimated 27 gigatons a year of CO_2e abatement needed to stay sub-500. They calculated that on average by 2030, using energy generation and carbon sequestration technologies we now know about, the abatements will cost an average of \$50 (40 Euros) per ton. And while 75 percent of the solutions actually cost money, 25 percent of the solutions they list are options on which emitters can actually turn a profit.

McKinsey's numbers are large and helpful. But they are also macroeconomic, and hard to apply to your day to day business. So let's break it down further so it becomes news you can use.

As we get specific about your business in The Post-Carbon Economy, we acknowledge that every business is different in both its key measure of output and how it creates that output. For example, in a utility such as Louisiana-based Entergy, the output is kilowatt-hours of electricity, generated by a carbon-intense mix of carbon-based and clean energy sources. In a pharmaceutical company such as Genentech, the output is drug molecules. Genentech's production chain is less CO_2e intense than that of a utility such as Entergy, but involves a much longer list of emission sources along the production chain. At Procter & Gamble, output is units of packaged good SKUs, Toyota's is automotive units, International Paper's is tons of paper, El Paso's is cubic tons of gas, Verizon's is voice or data minutes, and each involves various levels of carbon intensity.

If we are trying to measure how "carbon efficient" we are at Genentech, that means we are looking for the amount of CO_2e

ppmv produced per drug molecule. At Entergy, we seek CO2e ppmv per kilowatt-hour of electricity. For each company, "carbon efficiency" is stated in terms of the CO2e produced by each key unit of output. And the path that each company charts for carbon-efficient growth—that means how to continue growing while producing the same or less CO2e per unit of output—is the business holy grail of The Post-Carbon Economy. And that path's goal is nothing short of being perfectly carbon efficient. That means Net Zero Impact (or NZI), no net CO2e created in the production of your company's key unit of output. NZI is your business' ultimate measure of carbon efficiency.

Exhibit 10

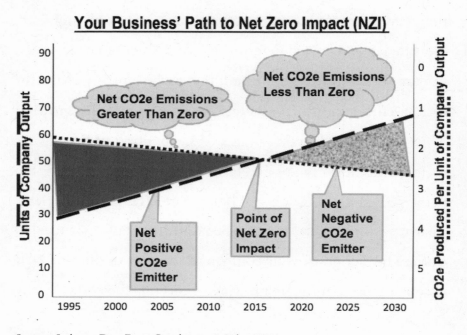

Sources: Industry Data From Google.com & Yahoo! Finance

In The Post-Carbon Economy, continuing to grow while cutting emissions means being your industry's most "carbon efficient" firm—producing less net CO2e per unit than your competitors. When your net CO2e produced per unit (i.e., tons of actual emissions less carbon offset credits and sequestered emissions), is zero, you're at Net Zero Impact, or NZI. The ultimate post-carbon competitive advantage is to cut net CO2e output per unit significantly below your competitors, even to NZI and beyond by cutting CO2e emissions, sequestering emissions when you can, and acquiring offsets for the rest.

So if it's not apparent already, winning the carbon efficiency challenge is secret #1 in *The Post-Carbon Economy*. Producing less net CO_2e per unit of company output—kilowatt hours or drug molecules or hours of service—than your competitors will deliver a significant competitive advantage. Since government agencies overseeing cap-and-trade regimes in the U.S. will be required to create a level playing field, your competitors will be dealing with the same carbon cost structure as you. As hard carbon costs get imposed by government mandate, your priority is to keep your business growing. The point of this book is to get you ready to compete when carbon costs rain down on all markets.

A sports story will help bring the point home. During a rainy and windy practice round in the 1976 Bing Crosby golf tournament at Pebble Beach, then-16-year-old co-author Jay Whitehead caddied for then-young PGA golf pro Fuzzy Zoehler. As the round came close to its end on the 18th tee, Whitehead, soaked through and trying to make conversation to take his mind off the terrible cold weather, asked Zoehler whether he had a trick for winning in the rain. Zoehler said, "Kid, only one thing to remember in the rain. The driest guy wins."

So Secret #1 comes down to this: staying the driest when it's raining carbon costs. Ultimately, NZI will be your best umbrella. Yet while NZI is within cost-effective reach in some segments, for other more carbon-intensive industries, NZI seems impossible or even suicidal. This book is your guide to how to succeed in either circumstance.

So the next question for those of us who recognize that the rain is coming is this: What are companies now doing to stay dry in a carbon-cost rainstorm, and how are they getting their organizations motivated to throw up their umbrellas? Specifically, what is motivating them to do the hard work to understand carbon emissions internally and in their supply chains? And what methods are they using for counting carbon? The answers to these questions are critical to understanding how to meet the challenge of The Post-Carbon Economy. That takes us on to Secret #2.

Chapter 5

Secret 2: Motivating, Measuring & Managing: The Business Process Layer Cake Model for Finding Opportunities in The Post-Carbon Economy

The concept of calculating a business' carbon footprint gained widespread popularity following the debut of Vice President Al Gore's documentary *An Inconvenient Truth* in 2007. By the time those involved in the movie accepted their Academy Award for Best Documentary in 2008, like moths to a flame, a swarm of CO2e consultants had been drawn to the business of carbon footprinting. By January 2009, *Corporate Responsibility Officer* (CRO) magazine identified 1,944 U.S. firms and consultants advertising their ability to help firms quantify theirs. By April 2009, a Google search of the term "calculate carbon footprint" would net you over 4.7 million hits.

The Carbon Disclosure Project, which operates by the principle "you cannot manage what you cannot measure," has taken visibility into companies' carbon emissions beyond the footprint measure that all those consultants are graphing. The CDP is a voluntary reporting program—a great strength because it teaches companies to measure themselves, and a great weakness because it's not mandatory. Since its founding in 1998, the CDP has counted on companies to find their own motivation behind reporting their CO_2e emissions. In 2006 and 2007 analysts and management consultants at AT Kearney also added momentum by reporting that stocks of companies employing sustainable practices outperformed those of companies using traditional practices by 15 percent.

Exhibit 11

Motivators for Voluntary Reporting of CO2e Emissions

For Companies	For Consumers	For Regulators & Policymakers
Internal: •Decision making & planning •Risk management •Benchmarking •Performance tracking •Develop products & promo •Pressure suppliers •Guide procurement •Remediate & offset emissions External: •Stakeholder communication •Emission trading •Product labeling •Marketing	•Understand how GHGs impact buying decisions •Differentiate "responsible" companies •Transparency through product labeling	•Establish CO2e allocation levels for cap-and-trade schemes •Establishing responsibility & ownership of emissions •Inform policies on embedded emissions in traded products •Transparency through product labeling

Source: Carbon Disclosure Project SP 500 Report 2008 page 40.

Beyond the internal and external motivators for companies, consumers, and regulators, the CDP has built participation with another tool at its disposal: fear. When Coca-Cola declared it would participate, so did Pepsi, out of competitive concerns. Same holds for direct competitors Exxon Mobil and Conoco Phillips, Apple and IBM, Microsoft and Oracle, ConEdison and PSE&G, as well as companies who saw their non-competitor peer companies reporting.

An added fear factor to force companies to report came in the form of nonstop cajoling from high profile CDP spokesmodels such as President Bill Clinton and German Chancellor Angela Merkel. The CDP is a master of peer pressure, with its reports and Web site chock-a-block full of examples from every economic segment. As a result, the CDP has successfully pushed for disclosures beyond Scope 1 and 2 emissions (usually the limit of a footprint analysis, which includes direct and indirect energy usage inside your company) to Scope 3 (which includes your company supply chain, disposal of company waste, external distribution, and employee travel). In 2008, 64 percent of the Standard & Poors 500 voluntarily reported their Scope 1 and 2 emissions, a number which will reportedly hit 76 percent in 2009, and near 90 percent by 2010. And in 2008, 27 percent reported their Scope 3, or the indirect emissions over which the company has influence (including employee business travel, external distribution and logistics, use and disposal of company products, and supply chain). Absent a U.S. government-mandated cap-and-trade system, the voluntary CDP has brought strong understanding of stakeholder motivations to create the gold standard for CO2e emissions reporting. As a result, the CDP is poised to form the basis for carbon reporting that will be used in the ultimate U.S. government-mandated cap-and-trade system.

In The Post-Carbon Economy, getting motivated to report your emissions is a prerequisite to creating value by innovating past carbon. While fear may have been the initial reporting motivator, most companies now see climate change is a bridge to commercial opportunity. In 2008, the CDP asked participating companies if they saw money at the end of the climate change rainbow. The results were impressive.

Exhibit 12

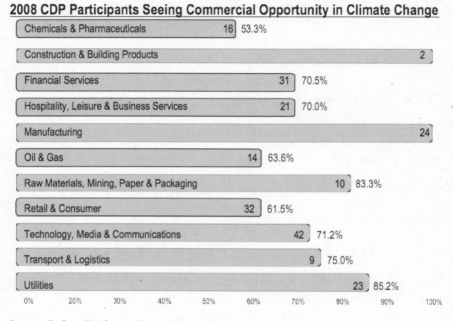

2008 CDP Participants Seeing Commercial Opportunity in Climate Change

Chemicals & Pharmaceuticals	16	53.3%
Construction & Building Products		2
Financial Services	31	70.5%
Hospitality, Leisure & Business Services	21	70.0%
Manufacturing		24
Oil & Gas	14	63.6%
Raw Materials, Mining, Paper & Packaging	10	83.3%
Retail & Consumer	32	61.5%
Technology, Media & Communications	42	71.2%
Transport & Logistics	9	75.0%
Utilities	23	85.2%

Source: Carbon Disclosure Project SP 500 Report 2008 page 54.

So while companies are motivated by both fear and greed to count their carbon, the actual process of finding the CO2e is harder than it looks. Tracking carbon emissions, like tracking energy usage, is a complex and difficult task that is rapidly being automated at major emissions points such as power generation and manufacturing platforms. While leading organizations such as Ceres and others have their pet frameworks for carbon footprinting, we have found that the process layer cake model has the most broad carbon footprint application. The principle behind the layer cake model is that energy usage and carbon emissions are best identified by looking at individual business processes. Within each process layer is a specific set of energy usages and carbon outputs that are hard to see using any other method.

Exhibit 13

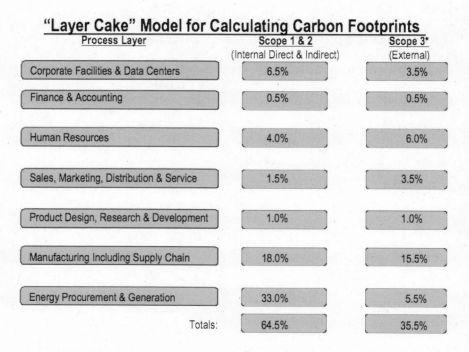

"Layer Cake" Model for Calculating Carbon Footprints

Process Layer	Scope 1 & 2 (Internal Direct & Indirect)	Scope 3* (External)
Corporate Facilities & Data Centers	6.5%	3.5%
Finance & Accounting	0.5%	0.5%
Human Resources	4.0%	6.0%
Sales, Marketing, Distribution & Service	1.5%	3.5%
Product Design, Research & Development	1.0%	1.0%
Manufacturing Including Supply Chain	18.0%	15.5%
Energy Procurement & Generation	33.0%	5.5%
Totals:	64.5%	35.5%

Scope 3 Includes: Employee business travel, external distribution and logistics, use and disposal of company products, and supply chain.

Follow the Carbon: The Layer Cake model for calculating carbon footprints, showing typical results for a company whose primary output is a manufactured product set. Note that over 1/3 of all emissions are in Scope 3, external to the company itself. In a non-utility service business, it is not uncommon for Scope 3 emissions to be 66 percent of total emissions or greater.

The main reason to employ a business process layer cake model for measuring and gaining control of carbon emissions is obvious: Management structures are most often organized along process lines. That organizational structure puts, for example, distribution leaders in a better position to count and manage carbon emissions from distribution than anyone else. Same thing goes for the manufacturing head, the corporate facilities manager, and the king or queen of the data center.

Another subtle but very important reason to employ the layer cake model is that within any process, a significant portion of the carbon involved resides outside the company's internal operations. In corporate facilities and data centers, many of those assets are leased from and operated by outside parties. In distribution, trucking and other shipping assets are operated by third parties. Similar story for outsourced services in manufacturing and other business processes. Since your individual process leaders all have visibility into their extended supply chain, they have the best chance to get visibility into their chain's carbon emission levels. That guarantees that your visibility into your carbon efficiency is not limited to the physical walls of your company.

There are many carbon footprint counting methods. In fact, we know more than 20, yet they all include emission data and conversion factors from a group of sources. The world's eight most prominent sources of carbon emission data and conversion factors are: the World Resource Institute (WRI) Greenhouse Gas (GHG) Protocol, U.S. Environmental Protection Agency (U.S. EPA), U.S. Department of Energy (U.S. DOE), Canadian Standards Association (CSA) GHG Registries, UK Department for Environment, Food and Rural Affairs (DEFRA), UK Vehicle Certification Agency (VCA), Australia's Green House Office, and the U.S. Energy Information Administration (U.S. EIA). Each maintains a robust set of Web tools that is easily accessed by companies seeking help in calculating emission levels.

Without getting too far in the weeds of individual carbon footprint calculation methods, we recommend organizing yourself to compete in The Post-Carbon Economy along your existing business process lines. That gives you the best shot at not only capturing all your emissions, but also managing to minimize the cost impact and maximize the competitive advantages you can gain in an economy when carbon is cash.

So now that we've established a basis for motivating, measuring, and managing your carbon inventory in The Post-Carbon Economy, what are the mechanisms that will govern the carbon costs that determine your company's competitive future? We know that government-imposed carbon costs will serve three masters: generating revenues to pay for remediating CO_2e levels, inspiring innovation in energy generation and carbon avoidance, and treating companies fairly by creating a level playing field. But how will you know what your carbon costs will be? Who will set the price? How will you offset your emission levels to beat your competitor's carbon costs? Just what is the deal with this carbon cap-and-trade thing that you are hearing so much about? What will the cap-and-trade schemes look like, and what opportunities will they present us to stay dry? For these answers and more, let's move on to Secret #3.

Chapter 6

Secret 3: Mastering the Ins and Outs of Carbon Cap-and-Trade

At its most simple, a CO2e cap-and-trade system is a market that puts a price on a ton of carbon emissions. Organizations are given an allowance of GHGs they can emit, and that's called their cap. An organization that emits less than its cap can trade the unused portion to another group that went over its allocation. In addition to direct trades of emission allowances, organizations can trade futures in their caps in order to manage potential future costs.

As it turns out, the U.S. is no newcomer to environmental cap-and-trade programs. Its Acid Rain Program successfully delivered 50 percent reductions in emissions compared with 1980 levels by setting caps for electric utilities whose emissions caused acidic rain to fall in the U.S. and Canada. What is more, nine U.S. states have active cap-and-trade systems in place that are generating revenues for those states. The Regional Greenhouse Gas Initiative, or RGGI, known locally as "Reggie," dealing in carbon offsets for companies in participating Northeast states (note: RGGI participating states include CT, DE, ME, MD, MA, NH, NJ, NY, RI, VT), executed three cap-and-trade auctions from September 2008 to April 2009 and raised a total of $44.5 million in MA and $14 million in CT, which got turned back into local green energy projects.[10]

On www.whitehouse.gov, the Obama administration's official Web site, the fifth bullet point of the administration's comprehensive New Energy for America Plan on March 1, 2009, read: *Implement an economy-wide cap-and-trade program to reduce greenhouse gas emissions 80 percent by 2050.* Rather than imposing the regulation himself, President Obama asked Congress to send him a bill that creates an emissions trading system, putting mandatory caps on CO_2e emissions for the first time. In response on March 31, 2009, the U.S. House Energy and Commerce Committee Chairman Henry Waxman (D-CA) and Subcommittee Chairman Edward Markey (D-MA) released their draft American Clean Energy and Security Act of 2009, a cap-and-trade program for GHGs. In the bill, the economy-wide cap would start at 3 percent below 2005 levels in 2012 and target cuts of 20 percent below 2005 levels by 2020 and 83 percent under 2005 levels by 2050. Similar to the regime used by the Chicago Climate Exchange, which we will study on the following page, the House bill would allow emitters to use eligible international and domestic CO2e offsets for compliance, with a supply cap of 2 billion tons per year.

Exhibit 14

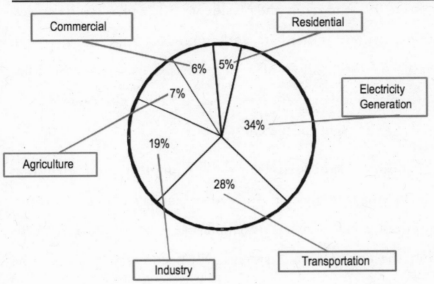

US CO2e Emissions Allocations by Economic Sector 2007

Commercial — 6%
Residential — 5%
Agriculture — 7%
Electricity Generation — 34%
Industry — 19%
Transportation — 28%

Source: Inventory of Greenhouse Gas Emissions and Sinks 1990
2007 (April 2009) U.S. Environmental Protection Agency

U.S. budget analysts estimate that the U.S. government would raise $645.7 billion from 2012 to 2019 by auctioning rights to emit CO2e, starting with $78.7 billion in 2012. To create inventory for the trading system, in his February 26, 2009, budget, President Obama called for the U.S. Environmental

Protection Agency (EPA) to get $19 billion to create a GHG inventory list, which was last updated in 2007, as in the chart on page 99. And while the president's 2009 plan has its critics, business threw immediate and significant support to it. On March 5, 2009, CEO of Chicago-based utility Exelon John Rowe was quoted in *Business Week* as saying the president "is very close to right on the climate plan."

The president expressed favor for a "cap-and-refund" plan that returns emission auction proceeds to taxpayers in the form of lower taxes. Nevertheless, the final program for use of proceeds from the cap-and-trade system will become clear some time after the CO2 reduction regime is in place.

The broadest geographic carbon trading program in place in 2009 is the European Trading Scheme (ETS), which at publication date was in its two-year testing phase. The ETS covers 12,000 factories in 25 countries. Each European country that signed the Kyoto Accord sets its own caps, then distributes allowances to emitters, who then can trade them. But the ETS has three big flaws. First, it excludes the carbon-intensive but politically sensitive transportation, homes and public sector from the limits. Second, the allowances are distributed without any cost to the emitter. And third, there have been widespread allegations that certain industries have been flooded with allowances, which makes the limits environmentally worthless. As a result, the two-year ETS experiment has come under intense scrutiny in the U.S. Most critics of cap-and-trade expect ETS to be revealed to be a system without either carrots or sticks.

By contrast, while the U.S. had no legal limits in place through May 2009, a robust voluntary carbon trading market had grown up. So while the final form of the eventual U.S. government-mandated cap-and-trade system is taking shape in real time, let's take a quick look the U.S.' predominant carbon trading market for some hints about what the future holds: the Chicago Climate Exchange (CCX), which is owned by publicly traded Climate Exchange PLC, the brainchild of the Chicago Board of Trade financial markets whiz Dr. Richard Sandor.

The CCX, as the only voluntary and legally binding GHG reduction and trading system for emission offsets in North America and Brazil, shows how trading credits, offsets, and futures actually works to limit CO2e emissions. What you trade on the CCX is not actually gas, but a contract called a Carbon Financial Instrument, or CFI, which represents 100 metric tons (110 tons) of CO2e. The CCX market sets the price of each CFI, and floats up and down with demand and supply.

As of early 2009, the CCX had 600 million metric tons of CO2e under its voluntary but legally binding cap-and-trade system, more than any country in the world. Companies joining the CCX commit to a voluntary but legally binding cap. In the CCX's first phase, 2003–2006, companies agreed to cut their CO2e emissions 1 percent per year. In the second phase, 2007–2010, members cut their aggregate emissions of six GHGs by 6 percent. A CCX member who has generated less than its allocation earns an emission credit in the form of a CFI, which is traded with someone who has exceeded their goal. CFIs are issued in "vintages," which is the year in which the emission reduction was realized. A CFI can be used in the same year as its vintage, or like a fine wine can be saved to be consumed in the future.

Founded in 2003, the CCX has three components. First, a trading platform which includes the CCX for direct credit and offset trades and Chicago Climate Futures Exchange (CCFE) for futures both of which execute trades among registry account holders who have accounts with one of the CCX's 19 clearing firms (e.g., Goldman Sachs, Citigroup Global Markets, Deutsche Bank Securities). Second is the clearing and settlement platform that governs the trading activities and processes transaction information. Third is the registry, which is the official database for Carbon Financial Instruments owned by Registry Account Holders.

Through April 2009, the CCX had more than 350 members including companies such as DuPont, American Electric Power, and Motorola, large cities such as Chicago and San Francisco, states and counties such as Illinois and Dade County, Florida, government entities such as the Amtrak railroad system, academic institutions such as the University of California, and farm bureaus involved in carbon sequestration such as the National Farmers Union and Iowa Farm Bureau.

CCX direct contracts are traded anonymously through the electronic trading platform that links to the registry. Members manage their emission inventory through the registry, and settle their trades either through the exchange or bilaterally among the principals. Monitoring of the securities trades is done by the Financial Industry Regulatory Authority (FINRA), and the emissions themselves are regulated by procedures set up by the World Resources Institute/World Business Council for Sustainable Development.

The daily carbon futures contract volume traded on the CCFE is on pace to increase significantly in 2009 based on companies attempting to gain a carbon efficiency advantage in advance of official U.S. government imposition of a mandatory cap-and-trade system.

While direct CFI trades can be handled either through the market or directly among counter parties, the carbon futures trades on the CCFE require a bit more infrastructure and anonymity to actually work.

Exhibit 15

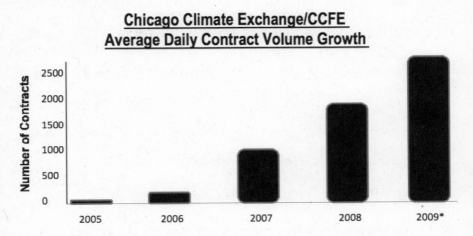

Source: Chicago Climate Exchange, *=2009 annual volume estimated based on early 2009 volumes.

Here's how a futures trade works, in four steps:

1. Customer A submits an order to buy, and Customer B submits an order to sell electronically through the CCFE Trading Platform. A does not know B's identity.

2. Both sides of the trade are reported by CCFE to the CCFE's independent clearinghouse, known as Clearing

Corporation, or CCorp. CCorp assumes the opposite side of each trade, maintaining the anonymity of both parties, and taking on the risk of the trade.

3. Trades are reported to each customer's Futures Commission Merchant (FCM), a registered brokerage company, which then deposits margin funds with CCorp to hold their customer's trading position.

4. The brokerage firms (FCMs) then collect money from their customers and provide reports on the trade.

The CCX has six categories of membership, each representing a key type of player in the CO2e market.

1. Members are organizations with significant direct GHG emissions that make a legally binding commitment to cut their net emissions according to a certain schedule.

2. Associate Members are office-based organizations that have negligible direct emissions that agree to offset 100 percent of their indirect emissions associated with energy use or business travel.

Exhibit 16

How a Chicago Climate Futures Exchange (CCFE) Trade Works

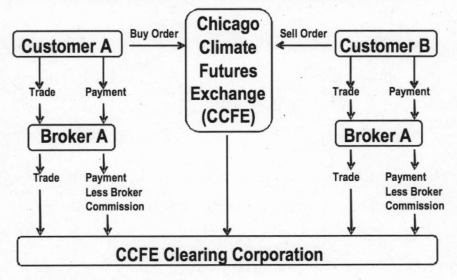

Source: Chicago Climate Exchange.

3. Offset Providers own title to qualifying offset projects that sequester, destroy, or reduce GHG emissions and sell offsets directly on the CCX.

4. Offset Aggregators gather offsets from owners and act as administrators of the offset sales on behalf of owners.

5. Liquidity Providers trade on CCX for purposes other than complying with CCX reduction limits, such as market makers and commercial traders.

6. Finally, Exchange Participants, are entities or individuals who buy Carbon Financial Instruments (CFI) contracts and retire them to offset emissions associated with specific activities.

To protect from so-called "sub-prime carbon credits," which include duplicate credits or credits based on a sequestration project of dubious quality, the CCX works with a list of third-party verifiers. Once verified, a project report is reviewed by FINRA before it becomes a tradable CFI. To make sure credits are not sold multiple times, each project is assigned a unique ID number in the CCX system.

While quality assurance is critical, CCX trading data so far shows that one thing is more important than any other single factor in ensuring broad compliance with a CO2e cap-and-trade solution: a legally binding requirement. The World Business Council for Sustainable Development reports that for every 50 credits bought on the CCX by organizations to comply with a legally binding emissions schedule, only one voluntary offset unit is bought.[11] At the CCX, a legal requirement is 50 times more effective than good intentions at keeping companies on plan. That means that once the U.S. government sets limits like in the case of the Acid Rain Program, compliance is likely to be high, and positive environmental impact significant.

Clearly, CCX and CCFE have allowed participants to learn more about trading carbon as a commodity. Participants now understand that the ultimate U.S. government-backed standard must result in both a sustainable for-profit trading industry and actual reductions in CO2e emissions. For that reason, CCX fans point to its success in building a self-supporting financial industry, however small, around carbon trading. CCX skeptics argue that the exchange's effectiveness in actually impacting climate change is limited and therefore the CCX model requires revamping.

Despite the criticisms, many analysts have assumed that the CCX/CCFE model will be the predominant carbon trading venue once the U.S. government makes cap-and-trade the law of the land. And since the CCX's and CCFE's parent, Climate Exchange PLC, also owns the European Climate Exchange (ECX), which trades the compliance certificates for the ETS, chances are high that both European and North American standards will evolve to look a lot like the commercially successful CCX and CCFE models.

Whether you are a direct seller of carbon credits, offsets, or futures, or whether you are broker, verifier, buyer, regulator, or other intermediary or advisor, in The Post-Carbon Economy, understanding carbon markets will be as important as it is today to know something about the stock market. Cap-and-trade establishes a market price and a market cost for a ton of carbon, just like the stock markets set a price for your company's shares. Carbon prices and costs are your keys to understanding your carbon efficiency, the ascendant competitive advantage in The Post-Carbon Economy. And a new form of cost accounting, which we call ABCC, will be your best weapon. ABCC is the topic of Secret #4.

Chapter 7

Secret 4: Carbon Cost Accounting—ABCC Unlocks Your Competitive Advantage in the Post-Carbon Economy

Accounting is powerful. When hundreds of cops with guns, car bombs, and big muscle failed to put murderous mobster Al Capone away, it took the power of accounting to finally nab him (ironically, on tax evasion charges). We know that no single weapon can beat climate change alone, not even mighty accounting. But without an accounting trick that can accurately allocate CO_2e-related costs to company activities, global business, the source of more than 70 percent of CO_2e emissions, will be unable to fulfill its environmental protection commitment. After all, for business in The Post-Carbon Economy, the most important impact of CO2e is not on the environment. The most important impact is on the bottom line. And accounting is how we get there.

But in carbon costs, there is no generally accepted accounting standard. And that brings us to a reminder: this book is often more about *what will be* than *what is*.

In The Post-Carbon Economy, we have a decided bias toward managing carbon emissions the same way you manage your business: by business processes. That is why rather than employing traditional accounting methods in The Post-Carbon Economy, we recommend you use an activity-based cost model.

Accounting's two biggest limitations are that while its rules are hard and fast, accounting often involves subjective judgments, and it is an art that is ever-evolving. That brings us to Activity Based Costing, or ABC and Balanced Scorecard, or BSC. In February of 2006, in order to better understand ABC, co-author Jay Whitehead took a Harvard Business School accounting course led by professor William Bruns, one of the two fathers of Activity Based Costing. Both ABC and its trendy 1990s accounting successor, Balanced Scorecard (BSC), assign more indirect costs or overhead into direct costs in order to get a more accurate picture of organizational resources used for each activity. While both ABC and BSC are complicated to apply and have many variants that are highly specific to the company for which they were developed, well over 70 percent of Russell 1000 companies have adopted one of them in some form.[12]

And while initiatives such as Prince Charles' Accounting for Sustainability, the World Business Council for Sustainable Development's GHG Protocol Corporate Standard, and its forthcoming WBCSD GHG Protocol Project Quantification Standard all aim to be the carbon accounting framework of record, all three fail to fit the whole bill. For one thing, while the WBCSD's protocol has some strong backers including the CCX and the U.S. Environmental Protection Agency, it only applies to accounting for GHG inventory and not to carbon offsets or credits, which means that it is useless for anyone involved in a cap-and-trade system. For another, neither protocol comes close to meeting the real-time decision-making requirements of modern management.[13]

So what's a post-carbon accounting executive to do? Our conclusion after interviews with more than 100 large organizations is that the winners in The Post-Carbon Economy will be those who use an Activity-Based Carbon Costing (ABCC) accounting regime that dives deeply into their organization's direct and indirect carbon emissions, broadly identifying the sources of carbon and energy costs and revenue-generating opportunities. ABCC uses cause-and-effect relationships to objectively assign costs, whether they are direct or indirect. ABCC in The Post-Carbon Economy will do different things for companies in different industries. For example:

- For energy-generating utilities, ABCC will include direct costs such as energy costs, as well as indirect costs of facilities and carbon emissions.

- For manufacturers whose products are produced offshore, ABCC will show that technology and productivity improvements and labor arbitrage have cut the relative proportion of direct labor and materials, but that indirect costs such as carbon emissions and energy used in transportation have increased.

- For natural resource-based energy producers, ABCC will add direct extraction costs as well as indirect costs of facilities, transportation, and carbon emissions.

- For agricultural producers, ABCC will both identify fixed and direct costs, as well as emissions costs from transportation and harvest and potential sequestration revenue opportunities.

- For IT hardware marketers whose users are often saddled with as much as 90 percent energy waste, ABCC will show labor and materials costs as well as direct and indirect energy and emissions involved in production, but can also be used to show product efficiency in energy and emissions.

- For financial institutions and other service businesses with diverse products and customers that have cross-product cross-customer subsidies and where personnel costs are greater than non-interest expenses, ABCC can add car-

bon emission and energy costs to indirect costs that are
attributed more accurately to products and customers.

The exact form of your company's ABCC will be, like all the
ABC and BSC regimes in use today, highly customized to
your business. If you want to see the net impact on your industry of imposition of a theoretical $10/ton CO_2e economy-
wide cost, skip ahead to chapter 9 to see what we call A Post-
Carbon Economy Model. As seen in Secrets #2 and #3, your
ABCC's accuracy will largely depend on the level of visibility
your company has into its own carbon emission and energy
usage cost drivers. And while your company's value chain may
include value added by suppliers outside your company (the
Carbon Disclosure Project calls these "scope 3" emissions, while
"scope 1" and "scope 2" are those direct or indirect emissions
generated within your organization), your ABCC is unlikely to
be able to penetrate into the activity-based carbon costs of your
supply chain. Bottom line, however, is the fact that having an
ABCC solution for your firm will allow you to create a carbon-
cost or carbon-revenue-based competitive advantage the size of
which will undoubtedly surprise you.

As we will cover in chapter 9's Post-Carbon Economy Company Model, the main assumption of ABCC is that you cannot manage costs, you can only manage activities. Then costs change as a result of the activities. In ABCC, your products/services/customers consume "activities," which consume "resources," which includes energy (which often involves CO2e emissions).

In traditional cost accounting, you arbitrarily allocate costs or capacity to your products and services without considering cause-and-effect relations. ABCC describes how activities or processes consume resources and generate or remediate carbon emissions. ABCC allows you to see which products, services, customers, and processes are actually profitable and which are most carbon efficient. With ABCC, our nuance is in adding another "c" to activity-based costing or ABC, which adds a carbon focus to ABC so you can see the carbon costs and carbon efficiency of each of your products, services, and customers. ABCC is the only accounting tool available to manage your way to the most carbon-competitive cost basis. As we will describe later, traditional cost accounting is too blunt an instrument to allow you to see the cause-and-effect of carbon costs in your products and services.

A side-by-side comparison of ABCC with traditional cost accounting shows you that you will no longer need to guess or arbitrarily assign costs, including carbon costs, to your activities. Rather, ABCC will allow you to manage your activities according to which are most carbon efficient.

Exhibit 17

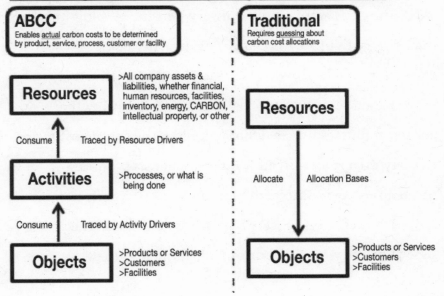

The Activity-Based Carbon Costing (ABCC) Advantage

ABCC
Enables actual carbon costs to be determined by product, service, process, customer or facility

Traditional
Requires guessing about carbon cost allocations

Resources
>All company assets & liabilities, whether financial, human resources, facilities, inventory, energy, CARBON, intellectual property, or other

Consume — Traced by Resource Drivers

Activities
>Processes, or what is being done

Consume — Traced by Activity Drivers

Objects
>Products or Services
>Customers
>Facilities

Resources

Allocate — Allocation Bases

Objects
>Products or Services
>Customers
>Facilities

ABCC allows you to peer into your activities, process by process, to identify sources of carbon inefficiency. As a result, you can identify which activities prove most carbon efficient or inefficient. This allows specific focus on creating carbon efficiency throughout the organization. ABCC will also easily facilitate the accounting surrounding the carbon-in/carbon-out trading activities resulting from your use of the coming cap-and-trade regimes in the U.S.

Traditional cost accounting assigns costs by volume-related allocation bases, such as direct labor. In our ABCC scheme, we capture costs not using arbitrary percentage plug numbers, but with activity drivers and resource drivers. Activity drivers and resource drivers are not allocation percentages, but they work the same way mathematically. Both activity drivers and resources drivers identify and track critical cost factors. Activity drivers identify how objects (such as products, services, or facilities) consume activities, and resource drivers identify how activities (e.g., processes such as sales or manufacturing or service delivery or distribution) consume resources.

To help you set up your ABCC system, we suggest you set up your activity and resource drivers in four types:

- **Unit Level Drivers:** These apply to every unit of product or service being produced. In law firms, this is hours of billing; in consumer products or retail, this is per product sold; in electric utilities, this is kWh produced. For each one of these units, the associated direct labor will be a unit level driver.

- **Batch Level Drivers:** These apply to each batch produced. In payroll or data processing, for example, the unit of choice is the batch, since paychecks or data statements are "batched" together.

- **Product Level Drivers:** These apply to every product regardless of the number of units or batches produced. This driver is especially important in tracking the number of product development or testing hours or costs required for each product, as in pharmaceuticals or products that require Underwriters Laboratory testing.

- **Facility Level Drivers:** These commonly apply to corporate facilities and other G&A-type costs. These are particularly useful for tracking the carbon emissions involved in a corporate, factory, energy-generation plant, or refinery-type facility.

In ABCC, rather than fixed and variable costs as in traditional accounting, we say that there are fixed activity costs and variable activity costs. A fixed activity cost is constant and assigned whenever that activity happens. A variable activity cost changes as the output of the activity varies in quantity, speed, or duration.

ABCC will allow you to see and manage carbon efficiency in a way previously unimaginable. For those unconvinced about the applicability of activity-based costing to carbon emissions, we offer a big-money analogy. This is the story of how using activity-based costing, Delta Airlines made a gigantic return on assets that, similar to traditional accounting's 2008 view of carbon emissions, had zero value. While a traditional cost accounting analysis rendered the unsold seats worthless, an activity-based costing analysis of Delta's unsold seats showed that the unsold seats were at the time costing Delta nearly as much as the company's expensive employee benefits plans.

So, a 1998 activity-based costing analysis convinced Delta to invest a "worthless" asset, a steady stream of unsold seats, in the then-startup Priceline.com. In return, Delta took a 10 percent interest in the fledgling Internet company. Fast-forward seven years. In 2005 and 2006, Delta sold part of its stake for a gain of $784 million, with the remainder worth more than $200 million even in the depressed market of early 2009, a total gain of nearly $1 billion. **After the Priceline sale, Delta's investment of "worthless" assets was worth more than 10 times the value of running their entire airline business for a year.**[14]

We don't want to oversell the ABCC carbon cost accounting advantage. But we don't want to undersell it either. As the CFO of Delta Airlines Ed West told Jay Whitehead, "The question at the time (of the Priceline.com deal) was could we afford to not take the chance? Unused seats may have seemed like waste or the cost of doing business, but that waste undeniably had a cost."

Granted, a Delta-Priceline opportunity does not come along every day. And even for those two fortunate partners, the outcome was uncertain for several years. Nevertheless, once a U.S. government-mandated price is established for a ton of CO2e via a cap-and-trade program, CO2e costs represent value that can, like unsold airline seats, be monetized in several forms, including for gaining a competitive advantage. But like in Delta's case, understanding where carbon costs lie and where the value opportunity exists depends on using an ABCC model.

Chapter 8

Secret 5: Innovations in the 7 Key Business Processes that Determine Winners and Losers in The Post-Carbon Economy

Typically, a book is a one-way experience. We write and you read. There is no interactivity. But this first edition is different, starting with this chapter. This is the chapter in which we spell out how best to manage your seven major business processes for optimal carbon efficiency. And here's your opportunity. While we spell out the major themes for best carbon practices in each of the seven processes, we're only two people...two very well-connected people, but two people nonetheless. We could never gather all the best practice data as fast as if we reached out to all the readers of this book for input, and included the best ideas in the second edition. And therein lies your opportunity to participate as a contributor in the writing of a major business book. Read on.

The remainder of chapter 8 outlines our principles of Post-Carbon Economy best practices for each of the seven major business processes. Once you've gone through it, we invite you to come to the book's Web site, www.postcarboneconomybook. com, to add your observations and experiences. The best will be included, with or without attribution at your option, in the second edition of *The Post-Carbon Economy*, to be published by a major publishing house. Those whose contributions are chosen for inclusion with attribution will be included as a contributor to the second edition. That gives you all the benefits of being a contributing author without the fuss and muss of writing 35,000 words.

So let's get into it. Secret 5 has seven parts. They are the seven key business processes that forever change once carbon emissions are priced.

1. Corporate Facilities & Data Centers

2. Finance & Accounting

3. Human Resources

4. Customer–Facing Functions: Sales, Marketing, Distribution & Service

5. Product Design, Research & Development

6. Manufacturing Including Supply Chain

7. Energy Procurement & Generation

For optimists, our business process predictions will be your guide to winning and wealth in the new age of carbon-cost recognition. For pessimists, especially those who doubt that business leaders will adopt *The Post-Carbon Economy* processes, chapter 8 is a preview of coming economic apocalypses, one business process at a time.

Secret 5.1 Corporate Facilities & Data Centers

If you are a power reader of technical environmental literature including U.S. Environmental Protection Agency releases, two data points will be very familiar to you:

- Heating, cooling, and powering buildings represented $272 billion, or 81 percent of all U.S. electricity expenditures and 74 percent of all U.S. electricity usage in 2009, with 38 percent being residential and 36 percent commercial. That represents 38.5 percent of total U.S. CO2e emissions, 21 percent from residential and 17.5 percent from commercial. To make these numbers even more notable, several estimates show that up to 45 percent of residential and 35 percent of commercial electricity is wasted due to poor insulation or wasteful heating or cooling practices (see www.buildingsdata book.eren.doe.gov, and www.eia.doe.gov for more detail on these statistics).

• In the same period, U.S. servers and data centers represented $6 billion in U.S. electricity spending, which is more than the power used by all color televisions and close to the amount of electricity used by 7 million U.S. households (about 6 percent of total U.S. housing stock). The CO2e emissions from these IT resources is roughly equivalent to that of the global aviation industry.[15] A 2007 SAP study cited in the company's broadly published ads found that in most business settings, approximately 75 percent of the server and data center power is spent when the computers are idle. Corporate facilities represent some of the largest challenges to easy reductions in carbon uses. First, residential and commercial builders have very little incentive to invest for long-term structural energy efficiency, and lots of incentive to cut construction costs. Builders actually own very few of the products of their handiwork.

Second, owners of commercial buildings generally pass utility costs to tenants. And tenant leases are often too short to include long-term incentives for utility efficiency. Third, it's very hard to track energy and carbon efficiency data on corporate facilities. Fourth, neither commercial nor residential building owners are willing to make energy efficiency investments with paybacks longer than 24 months. And fifth, neither capital nor incentives are broadly available to facilitate longer-term investments in energy efficiency.

On the data center and server side, by 2011 the U.S. EPA estimates that energy consumption by servers and data centers will rise 25 percent from its 2009 level to 100 billion kilowatt hours (kWh), representing $7.4 billion in annual electricity bills. Federal servers and data centers alone account for 10 percent of U.S. electricity use, for a cost of about $600 million annually. Data center and server energy use today is more than double the electricity used for the same purpose in 2000 according to energystar.gov. Most of data center energy use (>68 percent) is by volume servers, which includes the energy used for cooling data centers, which accounts for nearly half of all of the server electricity used.

For Secret 5.1, we invite you to send your observations and experiences in managing the energy and carbon efficiency of your corporate facilities and server/data centers directly to the pages covering Secret 5.1 at **www.postcarboneconomybook. com**. The best stuff will be used in this book's second edition.

Secret 5.2 Finance & Accounting

The Post-Carbon Economy flew in on the wings of more than $2 trillion in U.S., Canadian, and European Community economic stimulus to cure the 2008–2009 debt crisis. The vast majority of stimulus funds have gone to heal the capital markets, which got crushed in the 2008–2009 "short squeeze" on overly inflated real estate values and the debt security derivatives that hedged their value.

Ironically, the same brainiacs who brought us derivatives such as credit default swaps will in The Post-Carbon Economy be putting their inventive minds to the task of building new financing products and accounting routines to support the low-carbon energy revolution. Financial engineers will be using their ample experience in pushing carbon costs into the future. Like in the boom-boom years of easy credit, financial engineers will be creating new carbon cost-avoidance products to help accelerate their organizations' sales cycles. A classic example of how financial engineering will be used to accelerate product sales cycles is the way that electric car power provider Better is financing renewable car batteries for electric car owners. The company is using a cell phone contract model, i.e., sign a long-term contract and get the battery for free. This type of financing pushes the current cost of a battery out into the future and amortizes it over the life of the battery.

In the massive $800 million American Recovery and Reinvestment Act of 2009 alone, the bill's unprecedented tax incentives, direct spending, and bond and loan programs will represent significant opportunities for finance and accounting process leaders to reinvent their operations to thrive. A summary of the ARRA's alternative energy provisions shows up to $45 billion in alternative energy tax incentives, $26.8 billion in direct spending including $16.8 billion for energy efficiency, $4.5 billion for smart grid technology, $4.5 billion for R&D, and another $1 billion for other projects, and $7.6 in bond and loan programs including $1.6 billion in clean energy renewable bonds and $6 billion in renewable energy loan guarantees.[16]

In addition to financing and financial engineering work that will alter corporate financing processes, another coming boom is in carbon cost-related services. Because of the effectiveness of ABCC in finding carbon and energy economies, we expect a boomlet in three sectors related to ABCC. First is in software and related services to identify and manage cost and CO2e savings. Second is in Certified Public Accountants whose skills range to execution of ABCC programs within existing activity based cost programs or evolving out of allocation-based cost accounting programs. Third is carbon trading and carbon asset management, which will evolve as carbon is priced and market trading activity becomes more pronounced. And fourth is involved in structuring and creation of accredited carbon sinks and offset programs that can be traded into and retired. Many of these sink programs will be associated with existing forest products and forest preservation projects worldwide, and will become a significant sub-specialty in the carbon-related financial services arena.

Another development that we expect from the focus on carbon emissions costs will be the re-localization of outsourced business process services in IT, HR, finance and accounting, and call centers. While in a free carbon environment the cost savings from offshoring were significant, in a priced-carbon world, the business travel involved in managing the programs will narrow the savings sufficiently to force some programs back onshore. We do not see the services coming back in-house as a result of these new carbon costs. But we do see them re-localizing, coming back within physical proximity of the customer sites.

For Secret 5.2, we invite you to send your observations and experiences in managing corporate finance and accounting functions related to carbon management directly to the pages covering Secret 5.2 at **www.postcarboneconomybook.com**. The best stuff will be used in this book's second edition.

Secret 5.3 Human Resources

In The Post-Carbon Economy, we see three significant process impacts on corporate human resources. First, carbon efficiency initiatives will help save the cost-embattled employer-sponsored healthcare system, which in 2009 provided insurance coverage for 59.3 percent of Americans. The largest Post-Carbon Economy corporate human resources impact comes from unveiling the hidden carbon costs in employer-sponsored healthcare. Specifically, several studies have shown that up to 61 percent of medical costs are for expensive and carbon-intensive specialists rather than moderately priced and less carbon-intensive general practitioners.[17]

What's more, studies have also shown that specialists, for all their carbon-intensive high technology equipment, have only limited improvement in outcomes as compared with general practitioner-managed care. We expect that in light of both carbon efficiency improvements and the Obama administration's healthcare cost restructuring initiatives, referral to expensive and carbon-intensive specialists will be curtailed, a development that will help keep the costs of many employer-sponsored plans under control.

Second is a phenomenon we call "localized virtualization." Practically speaking, this means increasing the use of communications technology-enabled telecommuting. This practice cuts employee commuting and facilities costs, both of which are quite carbon intensive.

Third is the increased risk and carbon cost premiums applied to offshore services, long-distance transportation, and employee travel. We cover this a bit in Secret 5.2 as it applies to offshore outsourced business processes. Once ABCC reveals the true of carbon emission-based costs of long-distance relationships, we expect that companies will increasingly "localize" their operations. While employee travel is a Scope 3 carbon emission cost, its impact will increasingly be felt by companies compelled to count the costs.

For Secret 5.3, we invite you to send your observations and experiences in human resources related to carbon management directly to the pages covering Secret 5.3 at **www.post carboneconomybook.com**. The best stuff will be used in this book's second edition.

Secret 5.4 Customer–Facing Functions: Sales, Marketing, Distribution & Service

In customer-facing functions, we expect to see acceleration in both localized virtualization—telecommuting—and virtualized re-localization, meaning new technologies to replace business travel with customer-facing functions on customers' desktops. Before carbon pricing, the carbon portion of business travel costs was invisible. In The Post-Carbon Economy, it often will make the difference between a justifiable trip and replacing the trip with a teleconference.

In addition, as we pointed out in Secret 5.2, since carbon costs will be a concern for both buyers and sellers, there is a new and significant role for financial engineers who structure financing products to push carbon costs out into the future and make products and services more affordable. Often in The Post-

Carbon Economy, this form of financing will make the difference between winners and losers. Examples would include customer financing of railroad engines, long-haul trucks, electricity generating equipment, other carbon-intensive hardware, and long-haul distribution services.

For Secret 5.4, we invite you to send your additional observations and experiences in customer-facing functions such as sales, marketing, distribution, and service related to carbon management directly to the pages covering Secret 5.4 at **www.postcarboneconomybook.com**. The best stuff will be used in this book's second edition.

Secret 5.5 Product and Service Design, Research & Development

Because increasing carbon efficiency involves continuous product and service improvement, product and service design, research and development will be highly impacted in The Post-Carbon Economy. We see five major impacts on product and service design and R&D.

First, we see "de-carbonization" of products and services as a major trend. As we saw in the discussion of the Economic

Recovery and Reinvestment Act of 2009, the U.S. government has offered investments of several billions of dollars toward R&D for de-carbonization and reduced energy use in products and services. The trend toward de-carbonizing processes is one of the reasons we have our strong bias toward managing by process. Without a process-by-process focus, which captures carbon emissions like shingles on a roof catch rain, certain types of carbon emissions could be missed. In many product development teams, in fact, we see individuals being assigned as the "de-carbonization czar," in charge of eliminating carbon emissions costs from company offerings.

Second, the drive toward de-carbonization is part and parcel of the drive toward "dematerialization" of products and packaging. A recently famous example of dematerialization in products is in concentrated laundry detergents, which deliver 20 percent fewer CO2e through their lifecycle than non-concentrated detergents. In addition, in its packaging, Wal-Mart, which sells about 800 million units of detergent per year, has reported saving 125 million pounds of cardboard and 95 million pounds of plastic in its concentrated detergent collaboration with suppliers.[18]

Third, in materials science we see carbon earning its place in the materials equation next to weight, strength, and costs of acquisition and transportation. Materials science departments in six major U.S. universities polled by *CRO* magazine have now added carbon emissions-related coursework to their undergraduate or graduate curricula.

So Renault has re-engineered cars to accept rechargeable and replaceable batteries, and his Better Place has created a network of automated battery recharging and replacement stations. Another example is sustainable commercial carpet manufacturer Interface, Inc., which has redesigned its infrastructure around provide a lifetime floor covering service rather than around merely selling carpet. By setting a future goal of zero net carbon emissions, CEO Ray Anderson has engineered a "cradle-to-cradle" recycled product stream that feeds itself with waste stock while meeting the needs of demanding commercial customers.

Finally, we see carbon cost-related behavior changes becoming a bigger part of product design. To continue with the electric car example, Better's business model was significantly influenced by customers who warned of their "range anxiety" around electric cars. Because a typical car battery requires charging every 100 miles or so, customers were unwilling to buy based on the fact their trips would occasionally exceed the battery's range. A Better Place eliminated "range anxiety" by building a network of range-extending recharging stations into its business model.[19]

For Secret 5.5, we invite you to send your additional observations and experiences in product and service design, research and development related to carbon management directly to the pages covering Secret 5.5 at **www.postcarboneconomybook. com**. The best stuff will be used in this book's second edition.

Secret 5.6 Manufacturing Including Supply Chain

In carbon efficiency, manufacturing and the supply chain are among the processes most dramatically impacted. We see four major changes on the horizon. First is vastly improved visibility into the resource usage of companies' supply chains. This trend will leverage the already multi-billion-dollar supply chain management software industry. By layering carbon emission measurement capabilities on top of the existing software infrastructure, software providers such as SAP and Oracle can extend companies' views into and control over Scope 3 supply chain CO_2e levels.

A second impact is de-globalization, which is the process of dumping the carbon burden of a long supply chain. In some cases, components of finished products are associated with carbon footprints of such size and carbon cost that it will make sense to source the component locally. More than occasionally, companies will choose to re-bundle an outsourced supply chain into a vertically re-integrated operation in order to eliminate carbon costs.

A third impact is to give a competitive advantage to manufacturers who are proximate to natural resources and raw materials, because they require a shorter, cheaper, and more carbon-efficient supply line. China in particular sees this trend as its friend. In recent years, for example, China has bought majority shares in mining giant Rio Tinto, which gives Chinese government-owned entities close to the mine a significant edge.

Last on our list of carbon-based impacts on manufacturing and supply chain is a revamping of infrastructure assumptions, particularly around energy provision. For example, the new electricity "smart grid," which distributes power from a variety of renewable sources, will make proximity to conventional power plants less of a necessity. On the other hand, for users of biofuels, proximity to the source may be more important.

For Secret 5.6, we invite you to send your additional observations and experiences in manufacturing including supply chain related to carbon management directly to the pages covering Secret 5.6 at **www.postcarboneconomybook.com**. The best stuff will be used in this book's second edition.

Secret 5.7 Energy Procurement & Generation

Our final of the seven secrets-within-a-secret has to do with the most carbon-intensive of all business processes, energy procurement and generation. We see five aspects to the impacts.

The largest immediate impact in the energy procurement and generation realm has to do with the impact of U.S. government incentives and stimulus spending. Not since World War II has the federal government fed so much cash into national energy-generation and innovation capabilities. Altogether, including stimulus for conventional and renewable generators as well as energy subsidy for industry, federal involvement under the 2009 bill will total approximately $100 billion.

A second impact will be in the assumptions behind innovations in alternative energy. In a no-cost carbon world, for example, the primary concerns around renewable energy innovations would be cost and political control (e.g., avoid producing the energy in a nation hostile to the United States). In the Post-Carbon Economy, however, one of the primary concerns will be which emits the lowest levels of carbon. For example, generation processes that involve photon-to-electron-to-electricity are superior in their lack of carbon emissions to a process that involves combusting molecules to produce heat to generate electricity.

A third will be the financial engineering required to make new, more carbon efficient utilities, carbon sequestration, and energy storage financially viable. Pushing carbon costs into the future, creating credit derivatives, cell phone-type models for residential and commercial solar panels, and many other Wall Street innovations will be necessary to make carbon emissions go away.

A fourth includes innovations around carbon emission sequestration and energy storage. Both involve significant engineering challenges. A fifth, and perhaps the most politically wrenching of all Post-Carbon Economy impacts involves the gradual demise of the oil and gas industries. The common wisdom among fossil fuel pundits is that oil and gas will reach peak profitability immediately prior to becoming obsolete.

For Secret 5.7, we invite you to send your additional observations and experiences in energy procurement and generation related to carbon management directly to the pages covering Secret 5.7 at **www.postcarboneconomybook.com**. The best stuff will be used in this book's second edition.

Chapter 9

A Post-Carbon Economy Company Model

Writing this book has taught us one really obvious lesson: Telling the future of business is tricky, because business people think short-term, only trust retrospective data, and shun future predictions of change or bad news. Recent historical evidence of executives' near-universal inability to detect incoming business-destroying meteors is the churn rate of companies on the Fortune 500 list. From 1986 to 1990 the attrition rate was 30 percent, and from 1991 to 1996 it hit 36 percent. What's worse, those with a confident view of future cataclysm are often ignored. Back in 2005, New York University economist Nouriel Roubini was shunted aside, called a Cassandra and dubbed "Dr. Doom" by the *New York Times* for saying that U.S. home prices were riding a speculative wave that would soon drown the world economy. Shunted aside, that is, until 2008 when the debt crisis did indeed crush global financial markets. Vice President Al Gore spent ten years yelling into the wind about the Keeling Curve and the catastrophic future impacts of climate change before large numbers of people paid attention. Then, when people finally heard him, he won an Academy Award and Nobel Peace Prize.

All that is our way of saying this: After reading this book and starting to advocate the sure-fire certainty that your company's competitive position will change in The Post-Carbon Economy, you will face many skeptics. We can tell you authoritatively that all your Post-Carbon Economy skeptics are dead wrong. The Post-Carbon Economy is already here in its early stages, and is accelerating rapidly, changing the economics of every business, one business process at a time. As a result, it is our obligation to give you as many tools as possible to face down your skeptics and retire them faster than a used carbon credit.

This chapter gives you a model, complete with the most authoritative predictive industry cost data available, for finding your company's best place in The Post-Carbon Economy. To help you through the model, we ask the five questions that will get you to the finish line in identifying your carbon challenges and opportunities and charting a path to success. The five questions are:

Question 1: Where's the carbon in your company and what sort of reduction targets can you set?

There are more than 20 ways to calculate your carbon footprint, but we advocate following the "layer cake" model on the next page. We like the "layer cake" because its structure most often mimics companies' lines of management, making it easier to both count carbon and do something about it once it's counted. Scopes 1 and 2 emissions are those generated internally, directly by, for example, manufacturing processes, and indirectly, for example, in corporate facilities and data centers. Scope 3 emissions are those that are external to the company, by distributors or outside supply chain suppliers.

The example below is for a manufacturing company.

Exhibit 18

"Layer Cake" Model for Calculating Carbon Footprints

Process Layer	Scope 1 & 2 (Internal Direct & Indirect)	Scope 3* (External)
Corporate Facilities & Data Centers	6.5%	3.5%
Finance & Accounting	0.5%	0.5%
Human Resources	4.0%	6.0%
Sales, Marketing, Distribution & Service	1.5%	3.5%
Product Design, Research & Development	1.0%	1.0%
Manufacturing Including Supply Chain	18.0%	15.5%
Energy Procurement & Generation	33.0%	5.5%
Totals:	64.5%	35.5%

*Scope 3 Includes: employee business travel, external distribution and logistics, use and disposal of company products, and supply chain.

Follow the Carbon: The Layer Cake model for calculating and managing carbon footprints, showing typical results for a company whose primary output is a manufactured product set. Note that over 1/3 of all emissions are in Scope 3, external to the company itself. In a non-utility service business, it is not uncommon for Scope 3 emissions to be 66 percent of total emissions or greater.

Scope 1, 2, and 3 emissions vary greatly by industry. From Exhibit 19, you can get an idea how your industry segment stacks up against other segments that reported in 2008. In addition, this data offers the following six lessons that will apply to your company's CO2 emissions calculations:

- Utilities represent 75 percent of Standard & Poors 500 Scope 1 emissions reported in 2008.

- 62 percent of retail and consumer company emissions are Scope 3, or external and indirect, mostly having to do with transportation and heating and cooling of buildings that are leased from third parties. Scope 1 numbers are very low.

- 34 percent of financial services company emissions are Scope 3, mostly heating and cooling of buildings or employee travel.

- The Scope 1 emissions of building materials, construction, transportation, and logistics company are vastly under-reported in this report. If your company is in one of these sectors, you can expect to find very significant Scope 1 and 2 numbers.

- Scope 3 emissions of hospitality, leisure and business services companies are vastly under-reported in this report. If your company is in one of these sectors, you can expect to find very significant Scope 3 numbers, mostly from employee travel.

Exhibit 19

Emissions Totals by Emissions Category and Industry*

Sector	Scope 1		Scope 2		Scope 3	
	CO2 Emissions (in metric tons)	Industry CO2 Emissions Share	CO2	Industry CO2	CO2	Industry CO2
Chem & Pharma	67,700,343	4.0%	43,639,736	18.4%	1,083,249	0.5%
Construction & Building Products	160,353	0.0%	455,229	0.2%	NA	NA
Financial Services	7,944,549	0.5%	5,733,159	2.4%	80,595,479	34.0%
Hospitality, Leisure, Business Services	26,964,532	1.6%	8,492,249	3.6%	213,295	0.1%
Manufacturing	20,380,912	1.2%	23,693,784	9.9%	142,828	0.1%
Oil & Gas	148,633,073	8.8%	12,633,913	5.3%	73	0.0%
Raw Materials, Mining, Paper, Packaging	93,671.912	5.5%	43,218,381	18.2%	574,993	0.2%
Retail & Consumer	24,260,785	1.4%	44,426,351	18.7%	147,593,999	62.2%
Technology, Media, Telecommunications	3,594,843	0.2%	20,849,054	8.8%	3,917,625	1.6%
Transport & Logistics	26,772,368	1.7%	1,262,767	0.5%	NA	NA
Utilities	1,271,602,880	75.1%	33,202,010	14.0%	2,979,471	1.3%
Total**	1,693,686,550	100.0%	237,606,613	100.0%	237,101,012	100.0%

Source: Carbon Disclosure Project 2008 S&P 500

*=An additional 98.4 mil tons were reported with no breakdown

**=Excludes the disclosures of 7 companies reporting after deadline.

In parallel with counting your current CO2e status, more than three-quarters of large companies have set improvement targets. This trend certainly has accelerated in the wake of the debt crisis. By the end of the first quarter of 2009, 76 percent of Russell 1000 companies surveyed by *CRO* magazine in conjunction with its then-10th annual 100 Best Corporate Citizens List had established a present or future CO2e emissions reduction target. This number is corroborated by the 2008 Carbon Disclosure Project report showing that 73 percent of S&P 500 companies reported using the WRI/WBCSD GHG protocol to set a CO2 target. According to the CDP, the targets came in three sizes. Nearly half set annual reduction targets of under 2.5 percent, another 3/8 set goals between 2.5 percent and 5 percent, and the balance set emission reduction targets over 5 percent per year. The CDP reported that the most aggressive goals were set by four companies: Abbott Labs, 30 percent cut between 2008 and 2011; William Wrigley Company, 6 percent in 2008; JDS Uniphase, 20 percent to 37 percent over the next 18 months; and Advanced Micro Devices, 33 percent cut between 2008 and 2010.

We bet that exactly where you set your annual carbon emission reduction target will be a factor of three considerations. First, what are regulators requiring you to do? Second, how far can you afford to cut without damaging the business? And third, how much of a competitive advantage with customers, shareholders, lenders, employees, or other stakeholders can you get by coming out with a target? Only you can answer that third question for your company. But we argue that it is the third question that will offer you the biggest career and profit upside.

So now it's on to the final four questions of this chapter, which will give you the tools you need to set your target and get down to the business of preparing for The Post-Carbon Economy.

Question 2: Where's the money?—or—How does imposition of carbon cost impact your business' production costs, outputs, employment, capital allocations, profits, and position versus international competitors in the short, medium, and long term?

When you start to look for the true financial impact of the imposition of carbon costs on your company, nearly all companies start by looking at their energy costs. After all, annual energy costs for S&P 500 companies responding to the 2008 CDP averaged $749 million, or 5.7 percent of company operating expenses. But an overall average hides the wide variations among industries. Metals and mining companies pay 23.5 percent of operating costs for energy, while computer companies pay just 1 percent.[20]

Yet as it turns out, knowing your energy costs alone doesn't get you that much closer to figuring out how new carbon costs will impact your business outputs and profitability. Fortunately for you and for us, the environmental economists at think tank Resources for the Future have taken a number of deep dives into the question of carbon cost impacts on businesses. After wading through a sea of math, the RFF scholars have come to six practical conclusions, and have produced four very helpful charts based on a hypothetical yet low U.S. government-set $10/ton price on CO2e.

Their six major conclusions are:

1. The industries at greatest risk for output contraction in the short and long term are petroleum refining, chemicals and plastics, primary metals, and nonmetallic metals. These industries have limited ability to pass increased CO2e costs on to their customers, and therefore will be under the most cost pressure.

2. While short-term output and profit reductions in these highly impacted industries will be dramatic, adoption of new technologies will allow the profits to rebound completely over the long-term.

3. In manufacturing, the largest short-term cost increases of 4 percent hit petrochemical and cement makers, while iron and steel mills, aluminum, and lime products makers experience a 2 percent cost increase.

4. Among nonmanufacturing organizations, electric utilities, mining, and agriculture suffer the greatest impact, while the service sector, the largest piece of the U.S. economy, is relatively free of negative production impact.

While electric utilities are subject to virtually no international competition and are highly regulated, mining and agriculture will find themselves under immediate short-term cost pressure due largely to international competitors who are not subject to U.S. CO2e cap-and-trade –related costs.

5. Employment-wise, short-term job losses are proportional to output losses, but the remaining relatively small job losses are completely offset by gains in low CO2e impact industries.

6. Reductions in U.S. CO2e emissions that are offset by increases in non-U.S., non-European international emissions, known as "leakage," will be more than 25 percent. For the three most energy-intensive sectors, chemicals, nonmetallic minerals, and primary metals, the leakage due to imports and exports is over 40 percent. This leakage is a matter of concern for policymakers as well as for those who compete with non-U.S., non-EU producers, since they are unlikely to be under the same CO2e

restrictions as we are. "Leakage" points to the need for U.S. producers to be far more aggressive than their non-U.S. and non-EU competitors in planning for The Post-Carbon Economy. This is especially true for those in energy-intensive, import-sensitive markets.

If you recall from our earlier chapter, the good folks at McKinsey & Company predict that the actual cost of keeping the atmospheric CO_2e levels below 500 ppm is quite a bit higher than the $10/ton hypothetical CO_2e cost used in the RFF paper. But the RFF's $10/ton unit of measure is convenient, since the U.S. government will be under significant pressure to give near-term free carbon allocations to certain highly impacted industry segments in order to keep them from being price-shocked into dramatic contraction.

To back up their conclusions, the RFF scholars produced several very detailed charts, four of which we are reproducing here with RFF's permission, that provide you some pretty good guidance about the impacts you can expect on production costs, profits, outputs, employment, capital, and the impact of future technologies for each $10/ton of carbon costs. For brevity, we will spare you some of the detailed analysis of the impact difference between a $10/ton carbon tax (as in the last three charts) versus cap-and-trade. Regardless of some of the variance in assumptions, as of this printing, the charts on the next couple of pages are some of your most accurate predictive guides for what your business will experience throughout future stages of a U.S. government-imposed CO2e cap-and-trade program.

Exhibit 20

Estimated % Increase in Production Costs per $10/ton CO2 (2005$), Very Short-Run Horizon

Sector	Total Cost	Fuel Cost	Purchased Electricity	Indirect Cost
Manufacturing Industries				
Food	0.6	0.1	0.1	0.4
Textile	0.8	0.1	0.3	0.4
Apparel	0.4	-	0.1	0.3
Wood and Furniture	0.4	-	0.1	0.3
Pulp Mills	1.3	0.7	0.3	0.3
Paper Mills	1.6	0.8	0.4	0.3
Paperboard Mills	1.6	0.9	0.5	0.2
Other Papers	0.6	-	0.1	0.5
Refining-LPG	1.4	1.1	0.1	0.1
Refining-Others	1.4	1.1	0.1	0.1
Petrochemical Manufacturing	4.2	3.4	0.5	0.4
Other Basic Inorg Chemicals	1.6	0.4	1.0	0.2
Other Basic Org Chemicals	2.0	1.1	0.3	0.6
Plastics & Resin Manufacture	1.4	0.4	0.2	0.7
Artificial & Synthetic Fibers	1.6	0.5	0.2	0.8
Fertilizer Manufacture	1.8	1.3	0.3	0.2
Other Chem & Plastics	0.7	0.1	0.2	0.4
Glass Container Manufacture	1.3	0.6	0.5	0.1
Cement Manufacture	5	3.8	1.0	0.2
Lime & Gypsum Manufacture	2.1	1.5	0.2	0.5
Mineral Wool Manufacture	1.1	0.4	0.5	0.3
Other Nonmetallic Mineral	1	0.3	0.2	0.6
Iron & Steel Mills	2.3	1.3	0.8	0.2
Alumina Refining	2.6	0.8	1.8	0.1
Ferrous Metal Foundries	0.7	0.1	0.3	0.2
Nonferrous Metal Foundries	0.8	0.1	0.2	0.5
Other Primary Metals	1	0.2	0.4	0.4
Fabricated Metals	0.6	0.1	0.1	0.4
Machinery	0.4	-	0.1	0.3
Computer & Elec Hardware	0.3	-	0.1	0.2
Motor Vehicles	0.5	-	0.1	0.4
Other Transport Equipment	0.3	-	0.1	0.3
Misc. Manufacturing	0.3	-	0.1	0.3
Sector	**Total Cost**	**Fuel Cost**	**Purchased Electricity**	**Indirect Cost**
Nonmanufacturing Industries				
Farms	0.7	0.3	0.1	0.3
Forestry, Fishing, Hunting	0.4	0.2	-	0.2
Oil Mining	0.4	0.1	0.1	0.2
Gas Mining	0.4	0.1	0.1	0.2
Coal Mining	0.6	0.2	0.2	0.2
Other Mining Activities	0.7	0.3	0.2	0.2
Electric Utilities (incl. gov't)	8.3	8.2	-	0.1
Gas Utilities	0.1	-	-	0.1
Construction	0.5	0.3	-	0.2
Trade	0.2	-	0.1	0.1
Air Transportation	1.4	1.2	-	0.3
Truck Transportation	1	0.7	-	0.3
Other Transportation	0.7	0.5	0.1	0.1
Information Industries	0.2	-	-	0.1
Finance & Insurance	0.1	-	-	0.1
Real Estate & Rental	0.1	-	0.1	0.1
Business Services	0.2	0.1	-	0.1
Other Services Incl Retail	0.2	-	0.1	0.1
Gov't Excl. Electricity	0.4	0.1	-	

Source: Mun S. Ho, R. Morgenstern, J. Shih, Impact of Carbon Price Policies on US Industry
Resources for the Future Discussion Paper RFF DP 08-37 November 2008 pp 47-48

Exhibit 21

Estimated Effect on Profits of $10/ton CO2 Tax (Percent Change): Very Short vs. Short Run

Sector	Very Short Run (Quantities Fixed)	Short Run (Output Changed)
Manufacturing Industries		
Food	-0.39	-0.04
Textile	-0.80	-0.11
Apparel	-0.24	-0.10
Wood and Furniture	-0.49	-0.03
Pulp Mills	-0.85	-0.10
Paper Mills	-0.61	-0.11
Paperboard Mills	-0.63	-0.11
Other Papers	-0.47	-0.05
Refining-LPG	-1.59	-0.07
Refining-Others	-1.92	-0.08
Petrochemical Manufacturing	-2.26	-0.76
Other Basic Inorg Chemicals	-9.38	-0.19
Other Basic Org Chemicals	-8.64	-0.37
Plastics & Resin Manufacture	-3.70	-0.40
Artificial & Synthetic Fibers	-6.51	-0.18
Fertilizer Manufacture	-4.71	-0.36
Other Chem & Plastics	-0.34	-0.10
Glass Container Manufacture	-0.50	-0.10
Cement Manufacture	-1.52	-0.41
Lime & Gypsum Manufacture	-0.94	-0.17
Mineral Wool Manufacture	-0.51	-0.10
Other Nonmetallic Mineral	-0.64	-0.09
Iron & Steel Mills	-1.34	-0.21
Alumina Refining	-1.10	-0.24
Ferrous Metal Foundries	-0.43	-0.07
Nonferrous Metal Foundries	-1.36	-0.08
Other Primary Metals	-0.81	-0.11
Fabricated Metals	-0.51	-0.03
Machinery	-0.35	-0.08
Computer & Elec Hardware	-0.22	-0.10
Motor Vehicles	-0.33	-0.12
Other Transport Equipment	-0.28	-0.09
Misc. Manufacturing	-0.17	-0.06
Sector	**Very Short Run (Quantities Fixed)**	**Short Run (Output Changed)**
Nonmanufacturing Industries		
Farms	-0.21	-0.06
Forestry, Fishing, Hunting	-0.18	-0.04
Oil Mining	-0.11	-0.51
Gas Mining	-0.11	-0.63
Coal Mining	-0.30	-1.10
Other Mining Activities	-0.36	-0.05
Electric Utilities (incl. gov't)	-2.11	-0.14
Gas Utilities	-0.06	-0.49
Construction	-0.44	-0.04
Trade	-0.11	-0.02
Air Transportation	-1.11	-0.10
Truck Transportation	-0.56	-0.07
Other Transportation	-0.41	-0.05
Information Industries	-0.05	-0.01
Finance & Insurance	-0.02	-0.01
Real Estate & Rental	-0.02	-0.01
Business Services	-0.09	-0.01
Other Services Incl Retail	-0.20	-0.02
Gov't Excl. Electricity	-0.39	-0.03

Source: Mun S. Ho, R. Morgenstern, J. Shih, Impact of Carbon Price Policies on US Industry Resources for the Future Discussion Paper RFF DP 08-37 November 2008 pp 50-51

Exhibit 22

Effect on output of $10/ton CO2 Tax: Percent Change

Sector	Short Run Partial Equilibrium Effect	Medium Run Equilibrium Effect with Fixed Capital	Long Run Equilibrium Effect with Reallocated Capital (New Tech)
Manufacturing Industries			
Food	-0.38	-0.11	-0.12
Textile	-1.13	-0.51	-0.50
Apparel	-1.03	-0.18	-0.07
Lumber, Wood, Paper	-0.53	-0.32	-0.32
Petroleum Refining	-0.78	-4.72	-5.36
Chemicals & Plastics	-1.74	-1.11	-1.26
Nonmetallic Mineral	-1.20	-0.86	-0.94
Primary Metals	-1.57	-1.30	-1.21
Fabricated Metals	-0.33	-0.44	-0.43
Transportation Equipment	-1.14	-0.35	-0.27
Electrical Machinery	-1.00	-0.13	-0.08
Other Machines & Manufacture	-0.72	-0.50	-0.49
Sector	**Short Run Partial Equilibrium Effect**	**Medium Run Equilibrium Effect with Fixed Capital**	**Long Run Equilibrium Effect with Reallocated Capital (New Tech)**
Nonmanufacturing Industries			
Agriculture	-0.21	-0.06	-0.68
Coal Mining	-0.18	-0.04	-7.85
Oil Mining	-0.11	-0.51	-2.09
Gas	-0.11	-0.63	-10.04
Other Mining	-0.30	-1.10	-1.06
Electric Utilities (incl. gov't)	-2.11	-0.14	-1.17
Construction	-0.44	-0.04	-0.39
Transportation	-0.11	-0.02	-1.15
Services Incl. Retail	-1.11	-0.10	-0.06

Source: Mun S. Ho, R. Morgenstern, J. Shih, Impact of Carbon Price Policies on US Industry Resources for the Future Discussion Paper RFF DP 08-37 November 2008 pp 52

Exhibit 23

Effect on output of $10/ton CO2 Tax: Percent Change

Sector	Short Run Partial Equilibrium Effect	Medium Run Equilibrium Effect with Fixed Capital	Long Run Equilibrium Effect with Reallocated Capital (New Tech)
Manufacturing Industries			
Food	-0.38	-0.11	-0.12
Textile	-1.13	-0.51	-0.50
Apparel	-1.03	-0.18	-0.07
Lumber, Wood, Paper	-0.53	-0.32	-0.32
Petroleum Refining	-0.78	-4.72	-5.36
Chemicals & Plastics	-1.74	-1.11	-1.26
Nonmetallic Mineral	-1.20	-0.86	-0.94
Primary Metals	-1.57	-1.30	-1.21
Fabricated Metals	-0.33	-0.44	-0.43
Transportation Equipment	-1.14	-0.35	-0.27
Electrical Machinery	-1.00	-0.13	-0.08
Other Machines & Manufacture	-0.72	-0.50	-0.49
Sector	Short Run Partial Equilibrium Effect	Medium Run Equilibrium Effect with Fixed Capital	Long Run Equilibrium Effect with Reallocated Capital (New Tech)
Nonmanufacturing Industries			
Agriculture	-0.21	-0.06	-0.68
Coal Mining	-0.18	-0.04	-7.85
Oil Mining	-0.11	-0.51	-2.09
Gas	-0.11	-0.63	-10.04
Other Mining	-0.30	-1.10	-1.06
Electric Utilities (incl. gov't)	-2.11	-0.14	-1.17
Construction	-0.44	-0.04	-0.39
Transportation	-0.11	-0.02	-1.15
Services Incl. Retail	-1.11	-0.10	-0.06

Source: Mun S. Ho, R. Morgenstern, J. Shih, Impact of Carbon Price Policies on US Industry Resources for the Future Discussion Paper RFF DP 08-37 November 2008 pp 52

Exhibit 24

Estimated % Increase in Production Costs per $10/ton CO2 (2005$), Very Short-Run Horizon

Sector	Total Cost	Fuel Cost	Purchased Electricity	Indirect Cost
Manufacturing Industries				
Food	0.6	0.1	0.1	0.4
Textile	0.8	0.1	0.3	0.4
Apparel	0.4	-	0.1	0.3
Wood and Furniture	0.4	-	0.1	0.3
Pulp Mills	1.3	0.7	0.3	0.3
Paper Mills	1.6	0.8	0.4	0.3
Paperboard Mills	1.6	0.9	0.5	0.2
Other Papers	0.6	-	0.1	0.5
Refining-LPG	1.4	1.1	0.1	0.1
Refining-Others	1.4	1.1	0.1	0.1
Petrochemical Manufacturing	4.2	3.4	0.5	0.4
Other Basic Inorg Chemicals	1.6	0.4	1.0	0.2
Other Basic Org Chemicals	2.0	1.1	0.3	0.6
Plastics & Resin Manufacture	1.4	0.4	0.2	0.7
Artificial & Synthetic Fibers	1.6	0.5	0.2	0.8
Fertilizer Manufacture	1.8	1.3	0.3	0.2
Other Chem & Plastics	0.7	0.1	0.2	0.4
Glass Container Manufacture	1.3	0.6	0.5	0.1
Cement Manufacture	5	3.8	1.0	0.2
Lime & Gypsum Manufacture	2.1	1.5	0.2	0.5
Mineral Wool Manufacture	1.1	0.4	0.5	0.3
Other Nonmetallic Mineral	1	0.3	0.2	0.6
Iron & Steel Mills	2.3	1.3	0.8	0.2
Alumina Refining	2.6	0.8	1.8	0.1
Ferrous Metal Foundries	0.7	0.1	0.3	0.2
Nonferrous Metal Foundries	0.8	0.1	0.2	0.5
Other Primary Metals	1	0.2	0.4	0.4
Fabricated Metals	0.6	0.1	0.1	0.4
Machinery	0.4	-	0.1	0.3
Computer & Elec Hardware	0.3	-	0.1	0.2
Motor Vehicles	0.5	-	0.1	0.4
Other Transport Equipment	0.3	-	0.1	0.3
Misc. Manufacturing	0.3	-	0.1	0.3

Sector	Total Cost	Fuel Cost	Purchased Electricity	Indirect Cost
Nonmanufacturing Industries				
Farms	0.7	0.3	0.1	0.3
Forestry, Fishing, Hunting	0.4	0.2	-	0.2
Oil Mining	0.4	0.1	0.1	0.2
Gas Mining	0.4	0.1	0.1	0.2
Coal Mining	0.6	0.2	0.2	0.2
Other Mining Activities	0.7	0.3	0.2	0.2
Electric Utilities (incl. gov't)	8.3	8.2	-	0.1
Gas Utilities	0.1	-	-	0.1
Construction	0.5	0.3	-	0.2
Trade	0.2	-	0.1	0.1
Air Transportation	1.4	1.2	-	0.3
Truck Transportation	1	0.7	-	0.3
Other Transportation	0.7	0.5	0.1	0.1
Information Industries	0.2	-	-	0.1
Finance & Insurance	0.1	-	-	0.1
Real Estate & Rental	0.1	-	0.1	0.1
Business Services	0.2	0.1	-	0.1
Other Services Incl Retail	0.2	-	0.1	0.1
Gov't Excl. Electricity	0.4	0.1	-	

Source: Mun S. Ho, R. Morgenstern, J. Shih, Impact of Carbon Price Policies on US Industry Resources for the Future Discussion Paper RFF DP 08-37 November 2008 pp 53

Question 3: How do you use ABCC to find savings, revenue opportunities, and drive value?

In tracking your carbon footprint, we recommend the "layer cake" method where each "layer" conforms to one of your business processes, because that's how you manage your business. You have managers responsible for each business process, customer service, manufacturing, accounting, distribution, sales, facilities, etc. In carbon accounting, we stick with our practical bias toward process orientation by recommending that if you want to find out how carbon efficient you are down to the product, service, process, or facility level, your best tool is Activity Based Carbon Costing, or ABCC.

The main assumption of ABCC is that you cannot manage costs, you can only manage activities, and then costs change as a result of the activities. ABCC is cause-and-effect oriented. In ABCC, your products/services/customers consume "activities," which consume "resources," which includes energy (often involving CO_2e emissions). Traditional cost accounting causes you to guess about allocations of costs or capacity to your products and services without considering cause-and-effect relations. The power of ABCC comes from understanding how activities or processes consume resources and generate or remediate carbon emissions, which then allows you to see which products, services, customers, and processes are actually profitable and determine their carbon efficiency. With ABCC, our nuance is in adding another "C" to ABC, which adds a carbon focus to activity based cost accounting so you can see the carbon costs and carbon efficiency of each of your products, services, and customers. ABCC is the only accounting tool available to manage your way to the most carbon-competitive cost basis. Traditional cost accounting is too blunt an instrument to allow you to see the cause-and-effect of carbon costs in your products and services.

On the following page is a comparative diagram illustrating how ABCC beats traditional cost accounting in allowing you to get a clear view of your carbon efficiency throughout all your processes.

Exhibit 25

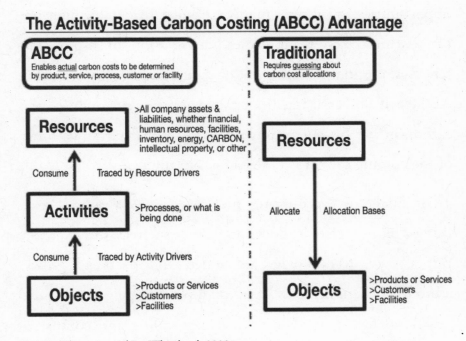

The Activity-Based Carbon Costing (ABCC) Advantage

ABCC
Enables actual carbon costs to be determined
by product, service, process, customer or facility

Traditional
Requires guessing about
carbon cost allocations

Resources
>All company assets &
liabilities, whether financial,
human resources, facilities,
inventory, energy, CARBON,
intellectual property, or other

Consume   Traced by Resource Drivers

Activities
>Processes, or what is
being done

Consume   Traced by Activity Drivers

Objects
>Products or Services
>Customers
>Facilities

Resources

Allocate   Allocation Bases

Objects
>Products or Services
>Customers
>Facilities

© Amit Chatterjee and Jay Whitehead 2009

Activity Based Carbon Costing allows you to peer into your
activities, process by process, to identify sources of carbon
inefficiency. As a result, you can identify which activities prove
most carbon inefficient. This allows specific focus on creating carbon efficiency throughout the organization. As a re-

sult, we expect that ABCC will allow you to quickly identify opportunities to become highly carbon efficient through use of new processes, technologies, distribution or production schemes, trading, remediation, or sequestration opportunities. ABCC will also easily facilitate the accounting surrounding the carbon-in/carbon-out trading activities resulting from your use of the coming cap-and-trade regimes in the U.S.

Traditional cost accounting methods tend to assign costs using volume-related allocation bases, such as direct labor. But as new technologies are added and overhead grows, arbitrarily assigning costs based on a percentage guess is quite risky, and has resulted in both career-ending and company-ending errors. In our ABCC scheme, we capture costs not using arbitrary percentage plug numbers, but with activity drivers and resource drivers. Activity drivers and resource drivers are not allocation bases but they work the same way mathematically. They are both used to identify and track critical cost factors. Activity drivers identify how objects consume activities, and resource drivers identify how activities consume resources.

To help you set up your ABCC system, the four most common levels of activity driver and resource driver are:

- **Unit Level Drivers:** These apply to every unit of product or service being produced. In law firms, this is hours of billing; in consumer products or retail, this is per product sold; in electric utilities, this is kWh produced. For each one of these units, the associated direct labor will be a unit level driver.

- **Batch Level Drivers:** These apply to each batch produced. In payroll or data processing, for example, the unit of choice is the batch, since paychecks or data statements are "batched" together.

- **Product Level Drivers:** These apply to every product regardless of the number of units or batches produced. This driver is especially important in tracking the number of product development or testing hours or costs required for each product, as in pharmaceuticals or products that require Underwriters Laboratory testing.

- **Facility Level Drivers:** These commonly apply to corporate facilities and other G&A-type costs. These are particularly useful for tracking the carbon emissions involved in a corporate, factory, energy-generation plant, or refinery-type facility.

One concept that gets dropped in activity based costing is that of traditional definitions of fixed and variable costs. In ABCC, instead we say that there are fixed activity costs and variable activity costs. A fixed activity cost is constant and assigned whenever that activity happens. A variable activity cost changes as the output of the activity varies in quantity, speed, or duration.

The beauty of ABCC is its focus on processes, which allows you to manage activities to control costs. Traditional costing is capacity and expense-oriented, completely ignores the processes involved in getting results, and answers the question "What do we have at our disposal to do the job?" If you look for carbon efficiency in a traditional costing environment, you will end up spending large amounts of time investigating processes one at a time. By contrast, ABCC looks at the causes of costs, including carbon emission-based costs, and answers "What needs to be done, and how can we do it most carbon efficiently?" But improving carbon efficiency is merely one of the advantages of an activity based costing method. Because an ABCC system focuses on causes of costs and critical success factors, it is critically important for continuous improvement in product and service design, quality, capital deployment, and distribution.

Question 4: Where's your competitive advantage in The Post-Carbon Economy and how do you map what your peers are doing?

In the British science press in recent years, much has been written about the Darwinian struggle between the Gray Squirrel and the Brown Squirrel in the gardens and fields of the UK. The Brown, a small, round, slow, docile, horribly cute and friendly species, is a favorite of British children's literature, and much loved by gardeners. By contrast, the Gray, an American import, is large, strong, fast, aggressive, noisy, mean, and murderously competitive with the Brown. In fact, the Gray has become so successful that in many regions, the Browns have been driven completely out of existence. To the horror of England's outdoor set, Gray has become the new Brown.

In many ways, we see the battle to be Britain's Top Squirrel to be a metaphor for competitive positioning in The Post-Carbon Economy. Indeed, we could plot the Gray's rise to supremacy on a two-dimensional positioning map, with one axis being aggression and the other being strength. If we drew the chart to have aggression and strength meet in the upper right quadrant, the Gray would be found up and to the right, successful, and the Brown down and to the left, extinct.

So it is in The Post-Carbon Economy with companies who have both a strong value-to-price ratio and combined near-or-below Net Zero Impact/low CO_2e cost ratios. In The Post-Carbon Economy, Top Squirrel will be in the upper right quadrant if we draw the graph on the following page:

Exhibit 26

The Post-Carbon Economy Competitive Positioning Map

Above NZI/High CO2e Cost & High Value/Price Ratio	Near NZI/Low CO2e Cost & High Value/Price Ratio
Hungry Squirrels *Occasionally Competitive --* #2 Competitive Position in The Post-Carbon Economy	**Top Squirrels** *Market Leaders --* #1 Competitive Position in The Post-Carbon Economy
Above NZI/High CO2e Cost & Low Value/Price Ratio	Near NZI/Low CO2e Cost & Low Value/Price Ratio
Blind Squirrels *Rarely if Ever Competitive --* #3 Competitive Position in The Post-Carbon Economy	**Hungry Squirrels** *Occasionally Competitive --* #2 Competitive Position in The Post-Carbon Economy

Value-To-Price Ratio — High / Low

← Above NZI   Net Zero Impact (NZI)   At or Below NZI →
← High   CO2e Costs   Low →

© 2009 by Amit Chatterjee and Jay Whitehead

As you can see from our Post-Carbon Economy Competitive Positioning Map, Top Squirrel products and services are at or below NZI and have low CO2e costs relative to their competitors. They also have high value-to-price ratios in other aspects of their value proposition, which means that to be successful your offering must have other market values than low carbon costs and low carbon impacts. It also means that if you have high value-to-price ratios yet are carbon expensive and have a large carbon footprint, you will remain a Hungry Squirrel. Same goes for you if you have a nice carbon profile but a low value-to-price ratio. But the Blind Squirrel role goes to the offering with a low value-to-price ratio, and high carbon costs and impacts. As the saying goes, even a Blind Squirrel occasionally has the luck of finding a nut, but he certainly needs to be very lucky to survive.

Objectively mapping your current competitive position versus your direct competitors on this positioning matrix will give you strong insight into your ability to compete in The Post-Carbon Economy. We stress the word "objective." We acknowledge that it's hard to be objective about your own offering. But doing an honest assessment of your position according to the map's axes will put you in position to be Top Squirrel.

Question 5: How do you best communicate your Post-Carbon Economy advantages to stakeholders?

The most important achievement in The Post-Carbon Economy is actual carbon efficiency improvements. But a close second is communicating your progress to all your stakeholders—customers and prospects, creditors, shareholders, employees, and communities and government. While professional practices in post-carbon accounting and post-carbon operations are early in their development, "green" communications professionals have been working their craft since the debut of Earth Day more than two decades ago. And green marketers have both the stars and scars to show for it.

Millions of words have been written and spoken about the biggest green communications stars: GE's Ecomagination campaign, Starbucks' Fair Trade and Sustainable Coffee production programs, Wal-Mart's compact fluorescent light bulb phenomenon, Toyota's Prius brand. On the scar side, nearly as much has been said about companies that overpromote alleged green achievements, a notorious practice known as "greenwashing." As a result, many companies today are afraid to communicate their environmental accomplishments at all, for fear of being accused of being greenwashers. In 2009, *CRO* magazine noted that the internal communications offices of nine companies making the magazine's 10th annual 100 Best Corporate

Citizens List refused to communicate their achievement for fear of being accused of inappropriate puffery.

But for the moment, let's put greenwashing to the side as a practice reserved for scoundrels, none of whom would possibly have read so far into this book.

Among communications pros' favorite strategies is that of claiming first-mover advantage. The first-mover theory goes that if you are first to successfully claim a leadership position, it's hard to unseat you. This theory has been debated long and hard by futurists and management soothsayers of all stripes— from John Naisbitt to Faith Popcorn to Clayton Christensen to Gideon Gartner to Michael Porter to Tom Peters to Peter Drucker. McDonalds was first-mover in hamburgers as fast-food, and maintains status as #1 in fast food. Starbucks was America's first-mover in high-end coffee house java, and maintains its lead despite recent strong challenges from many others. In 1995, Netscape was the first-mover in Web browsers, but has since left the scene entirely, supplanted by two late-movers, Microsoft's Internet Explorer and shareware Mozilla Firefox. Google was not the first mover in search engines, but has since claimed the market leader slot. Michelin was the first-mover in radial tires, and maintains market-share dominance internationally at the high end of the market. Nike, second-mover in running shoes after Puma, later gained dominant market share, and now splits the market several ways. United Parcel Service was first-mover in private parcel delivery in competition with the U.S. Postal Service, and now splits market share with the USPS and first-mover in overnight delivery, FedEx. Wal-Mart was first mover in U.S. big-box stores in non-urban centers, and now is the largest retailer in the world.

As for us, we think that as of summer 2009, The Post-Carbon Economy opportunity was early enough that the opportunity to be the first to communicate carbon efficiency supremacy is available in virtually every industry segment. And while claiming the first-mover spot is quite sexy, The Post-Carbon Economy race is long, and many industry segments will have multiple lead changes. We also think that in many larger and more energy-intensive industries—electric utilities, energy generation, construction, transportation, and IT—the opportunities are large enough to support multiple market leaders, carbon efficiency's Top Squirrels.

Whether your organization is a Post-Carbon Economy first or second or later mover, we offer the six important Post-Carbon Economy lessons to guide you as you communicate your improvements in carbon efficiency and competitive position.

1. **The Post-Carbon Economy places a premium on delivering five different types of stakeholder communications, rather than a one-size-fits-all message.** Each of the five major stakeholder groups—yes, there are five—sees carbon efficiency differently, and warrants its own set of messages, as follows:

   a. **Employees** will respond more actively to your environmental performance than any other stakeholder group. Hundreds of surveys of employees and prospective employees, especially those with Gen X and Gen Y age cohorts, confirm a direct correlation between a firm's actual environmental record and that firm's documented success in employee recruitment and retention. Gap, Inc., for example, reports that in a recent employee survey 75 percent of employees say that the reason they continue working for the retailer is not the company's employee discount plan or locations or benefits package, but its corporate responsibility reputation, especially its environmental track record. As a result of this and hundreds of other similar results by other employers, a green shoot industry in environmental employment branding advisors is now in full bloom.

b. **Customers** will respond to carbon efficiency claims when they are connected with traditional elements of a customer value proposition, such as value-to-price relationships or specific functional performance criteria. This conforms to our competitive positioning matrix earlier in this chapter, which aligns carbon efficiency with value-to-price ratios. And it goes without saying that being your market's most carbon efficient offering will pay the biggest dividends with customers if it results in an endorsement by Martha Stewart, Oprah Winfrey, Paul Hawken or "This Old House's" Bob Vila.

c. **Shareholders** will respond to carbon efficiency claims when they are correlated with traditional elements of an investor value proposition, such as projected price-to-earnings ratios, growth potential, or competitive market position. In communicating with shareholders or prospective shareholders, there is always a temptation to focus on the short-term—quarterly earnings or recent analyst recommendations, recent stock-price run-ups, or features on cable TV stock shows such as Jim Cramer's "Mad Money." We recommend forgoing the short-term in favor of a long-term message: Carbon efficiency pays long-term dividends, and is the earmark of a company investing for the long term, a buy-and-hold stock.

d. **Supply Chain**, including lenders, creditors, and landlords will respond to the message that you are investing for their long-term interests. Many surveys and studies in the supply chain management field and among lenders and commercial landlords since the 2008–2009 debt crisis have confirmed that these stakeholders are looking for the same thing—substantial indications that a partner has invested for the long haul. Carbon efficiency is the hallmark of the long-term player.

e. **Government**, NGOs, and community organizations are all looking for private sector partners that show them respect. We know that this statement might sound silly, blindly obvious, or even off-putting to those of you in the government, NGO, and community organization worlds. However, our statement happens to correspond to significant bodies of data that show that regulators and mission-driven stakeholder groups are most supportive of firms that work with them rather than against them. CERES, to name one environmentally focused NGO, is a vivid example of a group whose work delivers most benefit to those private sector organizations with whom it has actively and deeply partnered. The U.S. EPA is another. The list of additional examples is over 5,000 long.

2. Use real-life customer examples to tell success stories. Nameless composites are useless. In the post-Sarbanes-Oxley era, true testimonials have proven to be most effective in breaking through increasing credibility gaps.

3. **Use real numbers.** A strong example of success using real sustainability-era numbers is the railroad industry, which has gained measurable brand advantage from communicating that it can transport a ton of freight 438 miles on a gallon of fuel. In The Post-Carbon Economy, numbers matter. Use them.

4. **Use government and non-governmental non-profit organizations, or NGOs.** We covered this previously, but we know that this strategy pays significant dividends, so we are repeating to add more emphasis and detail. Non-profit NGOs exist for one reason: to help their private partners progress toward a mission. For that reason, private firm-NGOs partnerships are strong reputation-builders. Examples abound, but one is Domtar Paper and the Rainforest Alliance, two organizations that have partnered very successfully to build Domtar's sustainable product lines and Rainforest Alliance's market power. In addition, piggybacking on U.S. government programs is an increasingly effective tool for companies seeking credible third-party endorsement. For example, the dozens of companies that have promoted their participation in the

EPA EnergyStar program have nearly all gained market share over even less-expensive non-EnergyStar makes and models.

5. **Seek third-party rankings, listings, and market research that document your competitive position.** Historically, during early stages of dynamic markets such as IT, energy, business services, and financial services, leaders have emerged by steadily communicating their achievements according to publishers of independent third-party rankings. Consumer and business-to-business brand surveys often have pointed to the effectiveness of this approach to help companies climb their way into a perceived leadership position. Such rankings include *CRO* magazine's 100 Best Corporate Citizens List, the FTSE For Good list, and the Dow Jones Sustainability Index.

6. **Communicate early, as soon as you have a document-able carbon efficiency advantage.** This is the most controversial of our post-carbon communications recommendations, since it will raise a red flag with the greenwashing police. To those most frightened, we offer this: Waiting

may seem safe, but squandering an actual competitive advantage has been the death of many firms. Once you know you are in the lead, *carpe diem*, seize the day. While some second-movers have eventually gained the lead, to a person the late-movers will tell you their strategy was riskier and more expensive than being there first.

Chapter 10

What Next?

If you have read a bit of sustainable business literature, it is likely you have read carpet square inventor Ray Anderson's "spear in the chest" story. Getting a spear in the chest is what Ray said it felt like in 1994 when he read Paul Hawken's *The Ecology of Commerce*. When he closed the book, Anderson realized that Interface Inc., his waste-spewing, carbon-belching commercial flooring business needed to reinvent itself to be what it is today, one of the first names in industrial ecology. After much effort, capital spending, and logistically difficult process change, Interface has re-engineered itself into a paragon of what architect Will McDonough dubbed "cradle to cradle" production design, creating a sustainable stream of new products from waste stock of recently removed commercial carpets. Today, Anderson's firm uses a copyrighted set of what it calls its EcoMetrics to manage its goals of generating net zero waste and greenhouse gas. For example, from a high of over 160 million net metric tons of emissions in 2000, the firm in 2009 will emit less than net 10 million, despite significantly increased production. That's carbon efficiency at work. But for the record, lots of Ray's shareholders thought he was nuts. Many still do.

Unlike our true-green brethren in the sustainability community, we know that the Ray Andersons of the business world are few and far between. And no level of media myth-making will make large numbers of executives suddenly brave enough to take the risks that Anderson took.

But we do know this. Once carbon is priced, everyone will be required to participate in The Post-Carbon Economy. All of a sudden, once carbon costs are mandatory, the riskiest course is to do nothing to adapt. Regulation changes the danger equation. When the penalties for failing to go post-carbon are higher than they are to stay pre-carbon, that's when the competitive strategies we propose will come in really handy. Of course, whether you use our approach or not is up to you.

We are certain if you do nothing to adapt your business to post-carbon conditions, you will lose ground to your competitors who do. But be clear about one thing: Adopting post-carbon business practices has nothing to do with altruism. It is about competitive survival and success. By weaning your business off carbon emissions and the costs that are associated with them, you will be more competitive, period. It will not turn you into an instant greenie. But it will help you avoid ending up in the bankruptcy court system.

So while carbon costs are being added to the economy, what other impacts do we see around the corner? We are glad you asked. We see three significant carbon cost-related macro economic developments on the horizon that you need to be aware of, all of which will have some impact on your business' future competitive position.

Global Economies Will Grow Faster than We Expect, as Will the Pressure for Governments to Step Up Financially Painful Environmental Remediation Regulations and the Uncertainty Surrounding the Regulations

Back in 1999, the World Bank distributed a widely quoted and startling prediction. The WB's wise economists said that the world economy would grow 33 percent from 2000 to 2010, from $31.4 trillion to $40 trillion. But the World Bank got it wrong. By 2007 the world economy hit $54.3 trillion in size, or more than 20 percent larger than the World Bank had predicted, three years earlier than was forecasted. Today, Goldman Sachs says that the world economy will grow 360 percent between 2000 and the year 2050, from $31.4 trillion to $132 trillion. Included in that forecast is an assumption that the U.S. population will increase by 50 percent from 2000 to 2050.

If Goldman's economic forecast comes true, the climate change impact of such economic expansion will be significantly larger than can be offset by CO_2e caps that are currently envisioned by U.S., Canadian, European, Latin American, and Asian regulatory regimes.

The largest single reason for the increased climate change impact will be that large tracts of forest will be cut down to make room for economic activity. Forests, as it turns out, are the planet's largest source of carbon reduction. That leads to the conclusion that to keep atmospheric CO2e under 500 ppmv, government authorities in all major economies will be asked to make mid-course corrections to increase regulatory restrictions, mostly in the form of added costs. A sub-conclusion is that it will be increasingly risky to make significant economic bets on the direction of regulation.

A hint of this acceleration came on May 19, 2009, when President Obama increased minimum average gas mileage standards for autos sold in the U.S. by 30 percent between 2009 and 2016, to 39 miles per gallon for cars (from 27.5) and 30 mpg (from 24) for trucks. According to the U.S. EPA, the increased mpg levels will cut CO2e emissions by 900 million tons through 2016, the equivalent of shutting down 194 coal-fired electricity generation plants. The administration reported that the increases will save 1.8 billion barrels of oil and add an estimated $600 to the price of a new vehicle purchased in the U.S.

As for the increased risk of post-carbon economy investing based on fast-moving regulation, the April 2009 U.S. Environmental Protection Agency's biodiesel greenhouse gas emissions report is a case in point. Under rules in the 2007 U.S. energy regulations, biodiesel is required to produce 50 percent fewer emissions than petroleum. As a result of that 2007 rule, billions of dollars were invested in biodiesel production, mostly from soybeans. But in April 2009, when the EPA came out with its scientifically based studies, it reported that biodiesel only saved 22 percent in CO_2e over petroleum. In its calculations, the EPA included a factor for "indirect land use changes" on the theory that growing soybeans in the U.S .to make biodiesel could displace food-growing cropland. Crop growing would then hypothetically move to places such as Indonesia where carbon-consuming forests would be cleared to grow beans. Under the EPA's rules, such land use shifts would be included in the emissions profiles of both biofuels and ethanol. Biodiesel and ethanol industry groups were rocked by the ruling, arguing that if they are docked for Scope 3 indirect emissions, the same factor must be applied to petroleum producers. Without the indirect emissions factor, biodiesel industry officials say that their fuels emit 80 percent fewer emissions than petroleum. Since the ruling, several significant biodiesel producers closed up shop, and investment into the space stopped dead. In addition, in early 2009 the European Union slapped a tariff on American biodiesel exports. To add irony to insult amid all this regulatory turmoil, in April 2009, the market price for conventional diesel fell below that of biodiesel.

Increasing Scarcity and Costs of New Raw Material Feed Stocks Boosts the Popularity of Closed Cycle or Cradle-to-Cradle Production

When former NASA head and General Motors research leader Robert Frosch coined the term "industrial ecology" in his famous 1989 *Scientific American* article, he foresaw a trend that many companies are now more than ever claiming as their friend. "In an industrial ecosystem," Frosch wrote, "the consumption of energy and materials is optimized, waste generation is minimized, and the effluents of one process...serve as the raw materials for another process. The industrial ecosystem would function as an analogue of biological ecosystems." Closed-cycle manufacturing success stories such as those of

Ray Anderson's Interface, Inc., are combining with the increasing costs and scarcity of raw materials to cause many companies to redesign their processes as "closed cycle," or "cradle-to-cradle" operations. Cradle-to-cradle production is the opposite of the more familiar cradle to grave path, wherein product life cycle end in a waste dump.

Cradle to Cradle was the title of architect William McDonough and chemist Michael Braungart's 2002 classic book outlining the design principle known as "eco-effectiveness," involving reuse of feed stock and renewable energy sources. The closed loop production cycles advocated by McDonough and others mimic the energy production processes in a biological cell. Truth is, in business these closed loop processes also mirror biological cell loops in that they involve energy or material waste, known as entropy. At this point though, nature is much better at dealing with the large variety of energy and material inputs than business. For example, output of a plastics recycling plant is very sensitive to the availability of certain types of plastic feed stocks. Run out of one type and the plant and all the producers who rely on the plant for recycled material grind to a halt. The typical solution, huge warehouses of feed stock, while expensive, are becoming increasingly necessary as raw material prices move ever-upward and closed loop practices proliferate.

Since the beginning of the 2008–2009 debt crisis, dozens of companies' corporate sustainability and responsibility reports listed in the directories of *CRO* magazine and *Corporate Register* have documented acceleration in their use of closed cycle processes, nearly all cited as cost-reduction initiatives. A high profile example of the trend toward cradle-to-cradle production as a cost-reduction approach is in work of the Sustainable Packaging Coalition, whose membership includes over 400 of the world's largest packaging producers and consumables brands including Coca Cola, ConAgra Foods, Kraft Foods, McDonalds, Mattel, Nestle Purina, Procter & Gamble, and Starbucks.

The Rise of Super-Transparency in Supply Chains

When brand-name company products such as Cisco or Gap or Phillips Van Heusen or IBM or Fiat or Starbucks include components from an extended supply, the brand-name company pays the hard costs passed along by its suppliers. And while we have supply chain software providers to thank for our now-vast understanding of supply chain economics, we are still in the early stages of figuring out the corporate responsibility chain that resides alongside the supply chain. But on the environmental side of that responsibility chain, we are starting to get a clue. And once again, software is driving the supply chain transparency trend.

Earlier we covered how supply chain CO_2e emissions are most often counted as Scope 3 emissions, which are indirect and outside the company's control. As the pressure for governments to regulate CO_2e emissions increases, however, there will be far greater stress on the need for companies whose brands appear on the end product to be financially accountable for the Scope 3 emissions of their supply chain. Just as companies throughout the value chain in Europe now track the "value added" in order to collect and remit "value added taxes," or VAT, companies will soon need to track their "carbon emissions added" (dare we say that such a "carbon added tax" might be called a CAT?). The customer-facing brand name ultimately will be responsible for that "carbon emissions added" cost. As a result, supply chains are on their way to becoming super-transparent, driven both by impending regulation and the ability of software applications to track emissions costs along the chain.

A significant sub-trend within the "transparentization" of supply chains is the extension of the responsibility chain from manufacturing into the services sector. Noteworthy impact of this trend will occur in the transportation services sector, which accounts for a significant portion of commercial fossil fuel usage. Retail services also have significant exposure to responsibility chain exposure, since they are the endpoint in a long energy-intensive transportation and storage chain. The retail services sector also finds itself vulnerable to increased costs from the responsibility chain because it has proven to be an effective tax and tariff-collection channel for many government entities. Retail fuel stores, for example, collect nearly two-thirds of all energy taxes in North America.

We can manage what we can measure. Unfortunately, what can be measured can also become subject to a tax, a tariff, an offset, or a cap. And oftentimes, the brand at the point of ultimate customer sale becomes the government's collection agent.

Sources and Notes

Introduction

1. Resources for the Future, Competitiveness Impacts of Carbon Dioxide Pricing Policies on Manufacturing, Issue brief 7, 05.08.09 rff.org

Chapter 1

2. http://www.rediff.com/money/2009/apr/06india-to-see-7-point-25-percent-rise-in-salaries-this-year.htm

3. http://www.banknetindia.com/banking/subprime.htm

Chapter 2

4. www.algore.com

Chapter 3

5. www.iata.org May 31, 2008 press release

6. New York Times.com, March 28, 2009

Chapter 4

7. Mun S. Ho, Richard Morgenstern, Jhih-Shyang Shih, "Impact of Carbon Price Policies on U.S. Industry," Discussion Paper, Resources for the Future, November 2008 RFF DP 08-37, this and other citations used with Resources for the Future permission

8. Nicholas Stern, "The Economics of Climate Change"—
   The Stern Review, 2006, and Key Elements of a Global
   Deal on Climate Change, 2008

9. Eric Beinhocker, Jeremy Oppenheim, Ben Irons, Makreeta
   Lahti, Diana Ferrell, Scott Nyquist, Jaana Remes, Tomas
   Naucler and Per-Anders Enkvist, McKinsey & Company
   McKinsey Global Institute, "McKinsey Climate Change
   Special Initiative," June 2008, citations used with
   permission. McKinsey's data analysis is adapted from
   Yoichi Kaya and Keiichi Yokobori, eds., *Environment,
   Energy and Economy*, Bookwell Publications, 1993.

Chapter 6

10. www.masshightech.com/stories/2009/04/20/weekly15-
    New-England-helps-carbon-cap-and-trade-market-
    mature.html

11. www.science.howstuffworks.com/chicago-climate-
    exchange3.htm

Chapter 7

12. Kaplan, Robert S., and Bruns, W., *Accounting and
    Management: A Field Study Perspective*, Harvard
    Business School Press, 1987, ISBN 0-87584-186-4.
    Note: Robert Kaplan, Bruns' co-author, started
    promoting "balanced scorecard" as a more evolved

form of ABC starting in 1992 following Kaplan's Harvard Business Review article "The balanced scorecard: measures that drive performance," HBR, Jan-Feb 1992, pp. 71-80.

13. www.accountingforsustainability.org. Note: the GHG Protocol Corporate Standard was last updated in 2004, and is available online at www.ghgprotocol.org

14. www.fastcompany.com/magazine/39/changeweb.html

Chapter 8

15. www.gartner.com/it/page.jsp?id=530912

16. http://www.arc.gov/images/newsandevents/news/recovery/webinars/03-18-2009/Energy-Stimulus_overview.pdf

17. http://www.pubmedcentral.nih.gov/articlerender.fcgi?artid=1346463

18. Gert van Hoof, Diedrick Schowanek, and Tom C.J. Feijtel, Comparative Life-Cycle Assessment of Laundry Detergent Formulations in the UK, Tenside Surf. Det. 40, 2003

19. *New York Times Sunday Magazine*, April 20, 2009, p. 48.

Chapter 9

20. Carbon Disclosure Project S&P 500 Report 2008, p. 35

About the Authors

Amit Chatterjee has led one of the fastest-growing units at global enterprise software giant SAP and served *Fortune 100* clients as strategy consultant at McKinsey & Co. He currently serves as CEO and founder of Hara Software, the pioneering enterprise SaaS solution for Energy and Environmental Management for leading private sector and public sector organizations in the post-carbon economy. Amit is a regular keynote speaker at environment and corporate responsibility conferences worldwide and sits on the board of governors of the CRO Association. Amit's interest in business' interrelationship with the environment started during his involvement with the Global Reporting Institute, UN Global Compact, and at the Harvard JFK School of Public Policy. For his work in the Governance, Risk and Compliance technology space Amit was honored to be selected as one of Treasury & Risk Magazine's 100 Most Influential People in Finance 2007. Amit holds a bachelor's degree from the University of California at Berkeley, did his graduate studies at Stanford University, and graduated from Bellarmine College Prep School in San Jose, California. A U.S. citizen, Amit is married, has two children, and resides in Northern California.

Jay Whitehead has been publisher, owner, or senior business leader for more than 20 business media periodical and conference brands, including *PC Magazine*, *CRN*, *UPSIDE*, *San Francisco Daily Journal*, *California Republic*, *HRO Today*, *HRO Europe*, *HRO World*, and *NY HR Week*. He currently serves as president and publisher at Crossing Media LLC, and publishes four business magazines including *CRO* magazine, home of the 100 Best Corporate Citizens List, chairs the CRO Summits in the U.S. and Europe, and is on the board of governors of the CRO Association. Jay appears regularly on CNBC, NBC Nightly News, MSNBC, and has maintained a syndicated national radio show on Business America Radio. Jay has founded several business associations including the HRO Association and the CRO Association. In addition to media ventures, Jay founded pioneering online HR outsourcing provider EmployeeService.com, for which he raised more than $20 million in venture capital. Jay serves on boards of directors of several companies, including Montreal-based Rideau Recognition. He holds a Bachelor of Arts in History and Russian from the University of California at Los Angeles, a Strategic Finance certificate from the Harvard Business School, and graduated from Carmel High School in Carmel, California. A dual U.S.-French citizen, Jay is married, has three children, and resides in New Jersey.